The Land of Christ

The Land of Christ

A Palestinian Cry

YOHANNA KATANACHO

with a foreword by Bishara Awad

PICKWICK *Publications* · Eugene, Oregon

THE LAND OF CHRIST
A Palestinian Cry

Pickwick Publications
An Imprint of Wipf and Stock Publishers
199 W. 8th Ave., Suite 3
Eugene, OR 97401

www.wipfandstock.com

ISBN 13: 978-1-62032-664-0

Cataloging-in-Publication data:

Katanacho, Yohanna.

The land of Christ : a Palestinian cry / Yohanna Katanacho ; foreword by Bishara Awad.

xiv + 96 pp. ; 23 cm—Includes bibliographical references.

ISBN 13: 978-1-62032-664-0

1. Arab-Israeli conflict—Religious aspects. 2. Land tenure—Religious aspects. 3. Land tenure—Biblical teaching. I. Awad, Bishara. II. Title.

DS119.7 .K38 2013

Manufactured in the USA

Contents

Foreword

"THE LAND OF CHRIST: A Palestinian Cry," by Rev. Dr. Yohanna Katanacho is the book of the day. It comes at an important time, a time when the Palestinians, after years of waiting and counting on the international community to do them justice, have realized that that community never did come even close to granting them any justice.

The book is timely since the Palestinians have been under Israeli military occupation for over forty-four years and there is still no sign of lifting the yoke. The book comes just as the Palestinian Church has issued the Kairos Document, which calls for a moment of truth to bring peace and justice to the Palestinians. The book also comes after the conference "Christ at the Checkpoint" as Evangelical Churches worldwide seek to find hope, peace, and justice. There are also cries among many other Palestinians who have been working for years without a sign of hope, but who have never given up seeking peace and living in hope. Groups like Holy Land Trust, Sabeel, Wiam, Dar El Nadweh, El-Haq, and many others have all played a part in the struggle for peace and justice.

The book comes as Palestinian Authority president, Mr. Mahmoud Abbas, returns from the UN in September 2011 following the bid for a Palestinian State. This book comes at the height of the Arab Spring, as Middle East nations are protesting against leaders who were for the most part looking after their own interests rather than listening to the cries of their people and the suffering of the Palestinians. The book is timely as Israeli leaders continue to give little or no concern to matters of peace and justice.

The book sheds light on many questions and concerns on both sides of the Arab-Israeli conflict. The author, Dr. Kanatacho, is certainly not shy in giving us his testimony and deep conviction of faith in a Savior, Jesus Christ. It is not only a matter of faith, but also a matter of how faith in the Redeemer can be applied in daily encounters with the community, the enemy, the oppressed, and all religious people. For Dr. Kanatacho there is no separation between faith and everyday activities. It is very obvious that faith in a Redeemer leads a person to do "justice, love mercy, and to walk humbly with God"—Micah 6:8. As we look up to this Redeemer, we realize that he is righteous and a God of justice (Isa 30:18). As a follower of God, Dr. Katanacho wants to see changes on the ground, changes toward fairness and justice for all.

Dr. Katanacho rightly presents us with a suffering land and a suffering people. The land is the Holy Land; the people are the Palestinians and Israelis. A close look at the land of Palestine and its people reveals a suffering community. Consider hundreds of women weeping because their husbands or sons were shot dead or are in Israeli jails. Consider the apartheid wall that separates families and farmers from their farms. Consider the frustration of people losing their land as it is confiscated to build Israeli settlements. Consider the humiliations the Palestinians receive at the checkpoints. The list continues, and the suffering escalates.

There are obvious causes for the suffering, the occupation, the oppression, the oppressors, and most of all "sin entered the land." The author does not leave us in despair. Like the author himself, one can find peace with God, contextualized in loving the oppressed, the thief, the enemy, and the sinner. For Katanacho the centrality of Christ and his redeeming power are the most important issues. Yes there is suffering, but there is also a Redeemer. There is the second Adam who will redeem the land and the people who are in the land. With this Redeemer on your side, you can resist evil and rest in the Lord. Following the Redeemer Jesus, one can love the enemy, and look at all people as equal, even the sinner and oppressor. Followers of the Redeemer give value to every human being, child, young or old, an enemy or a thief. Yes, according to Katanacho, one can love the enemy and go the "second mile." Following this path and mode of thinking one can truly find hope. This is how Hagar was not left to suffer, but was redeemed. In God's eyes there are no second-class citizens. There is no doubt in the mind of the author that the Palestinians, who are the natives of the land, are loved by God. Immanuel came for them as well as for the rest of the world, to love and to redeem.

The Kairos Document is a message for the nations and the powers to embark on change. It is a cry for leaders to do justice and seek God's righteousness. It is a journey for people to follow in order to end up with peace, rest and hope. As the people of God come together, things will change.

Dr. Katanacho wrote this book because he is seeking positive results. Suffering will come to an end, tears will dry, and the land will be healed. Suffering is never an end, but hope, love, and a new dawn are on the horizon. The Kairos Document is thus an instrument in making a path straight. Dr. Katanacho bases this document on clear biblical principles.

I personally want to thank Rev. Dr. Katanacho for this wonderful work that I know will bring honor and glory to God.

Dr. Bishara Awad
Founder of Bethlehem Bible College

Preface

I AM WRITING THIS book as a theologian, but the subject is more than a theological study. It is also very personal—it is my life. For those of us who live in the Middle East, in Israel (or Palestine) specifically, theology is an integral part of our lives. Even the ordinary business of buying or selling land has theological significance among people who claim certain privilege based on divine right.

Theology affects every aspect of my life, as the theologies of the three major world religions (Christianity, Judaism, and Islam) influence the mentality and behavior of each community with numerous religious practices and customs. In Jerusalem, religious dietary laws dictate what I can and cannot eat in many restaurants. As I walk through the streets or visit the holy sites of old Jerusalem, I must always be aware of my dress and behavior in order not to offend another's religious conviction. I dare not drive my car through an Orthodox Jewish neighborhood from Friday evening to Saturday (Shabbat) as I would not only offend, but also risk having my car stoned. Carrying a bottle of wine openly through a Muslim neighborhood would be offensive, as would eating in public during the days of Ramadan when everyone is fasting.[1]

My own life, as a follower of Jesus Christ in Israel/Palestine, has been shaped by several theological turning points: my conversion; my struggle with loving my enemies; my pursuit of truth in a country full of hatred, war, and bloodshed. Each was a defining moment based on a major theological question for which I needed an answer. As a result, I start in this book with my personal story but I later present my theological study. The second part is more academic. Both parts are equally important.

---

1. For more information about the Christian and Ramadan, see Yohanna Katanacho, "Christian and Ramadan," 102–6.

This book, then, attempts to address the following concerns: the context of my conversion and my relationship with the "enemy"; the theology of the land and my relationship with fellow believers who may overlook the Palestinian Church; my experience living under the Israeli occupation; my involvement with, and contribution to, the Palestinian Kairos Document; and finally, what is our hope?

My purpose was to write a theological book and, in so doing, address the vexing questions so significant to my own life and to the theology of the land.

Acknowledgments

Writing this book would not have been possible without the wonderful support that I had from my wife Dina and my three boys: Immanuel, Jonathan, and Christopher.

Furthermore, I thank Dr. Bishara Awad, the President Emeritus of Bethlehem Bible College, who has been supportive through his prayers and kind words. He has always been a great model of godliness for me throughout the years. I also thank Rev. Dr. Jack Sara, President of Bethlehem Bible College, for his enthusiasm and help. The faculty of Bethlehem Bible College, especially Rev. Alex Awad, Rev. Colin Chapman, Dr. Salim Munayer, and Mr. Munther Isaac, have enriched my understanding of the theology of the land and Palestinian contextual theology. I thank them for their interactions and their honest feedback.

I also thank the authors of the Palestinian Kairos Document. They have helped me to relate to my brothers and sisters in other churches and have enhanced my ability to connect between my context and my faith. Their commitment to God, to the church, and to biblical peace and justice will continue to inspire me.

Last but not least, special thanks to Beverley Timgren, Botrus Mansour, and Soheir Girgis who helped by reading the manuscript and by giving comments throughout the process. Soheir has reviewed all the biblical references and has provided significant editorial help.

one

The Context

ALL THEOLOGY IS CONTEXTUAL. We look at a text from a particular point of view, a particular interest, and highlight some aspects of the text. It is important, then, to study theology in community, interacting with and learning from one another, for individuals cannot escape the peril of creating a canon within a canon. Each interpretation tends toward a particular angle of the truth.

Furthermore, it is important to study theology with humility, to be willing to listen to and learn from one another. Humility and community are especially important when it comes to the "theology of the land" and the theological ways in which we perceive the modern state of Israel.

Disagreements may be very personal and emotional and may influence the way Palestinians and Israelis, Christian Zionists and covenant theologians relate to one another. A theological assertion such as "God gave the land to Israel" has not only theological, but also military, economic, and political implications. In this book, I will address this assertion from my perspective as an evangelical Palestinian Arab Christian. First, though, an explanation of my background is important for the reader to understand the context of my presentation and interpretation of biblical texts.

EVANGELICAL CHRISTIAN

For the sake of simplicity, I use the term "evangelical" to refer to people in Israel/Palestine who are followers of Jesus Christ, affirm the need for personal conversion, and accept the authority of the Bible. Good theology is embedded in a personal relationship with God, so I must begin with my own conversion story and acknowledgement of the authority of the Bible, as one living in a culture of hatred and a land torn by conflict.

I was born in Jerusalem, in June 1967, during the Arab–Israeli war known as the "Six-Day War." Due to the curfew imposed on East Jerusalem, my mother could not leave the hospital. However, my father risked his life to bring us home and despite the bomb that exploded next to the entrance of our home, tragically killing our neighbor, we arrived home safely. This is how my life began, and ever since, I have lived with conflict and wars motivated by politics and religion.

I grew up in Jerusalem, a city full of religious people—Jews, Muslims, and Christians—who often walk along the same streets, distinguishable by their dress. It is common to see the robe and turban of a Muslim sheikh, the long dress and head scarf of a Muslim woman, the black coat and hat of an Orthodox Jewish man, and the modest dress and head covering of an Orthodox Jewish woman. There are priests and nuns of various religious orders and others, both religious and secular, who come from all over the world. My family is part of this diversity.

My mother is an Armenian Catholic. Her parents fled from Armenia to seek refuge in Jerusalem in 1915, having lost many relatives in massacres rooted in hatred and religious persecution. Although my mother wanted to become a nun, she fell in love with my father, a Roman Catholic Palestinian Arab. He and most of his family lost their homes in Ramle (near Tel Aviv) during the 1948 war and sought refuge in Jerusalem. Although both of my parents suffered the loss and hardship of war and persecution, I never saw hatred in them toward anyone. My parents taught me well; however, I re-fused the teachings of the church. As a teenager I was an atheist and actively led a student group promoting atheism at Bethlehem University (in the West Bank). My studies in chemistry, biology, and philosophy reinforced my atheistic beliefs, and the philosophy of atheism was realized practically in my life; I lived as though God did not exist. I was influenced by the im-morality of my friends and by my desire to live free of religion and ethics. I also participated in many ungodly activities that I am now ashamed to mention. However, much to my surprise, God intervened in my life with his grace.

Early one morning in 1986, I awoke to the sound of the church bells of Jerusalem. It was 3:00 a.m. I opened my eyes and felt a strange sensation like air penetrating my body! And then, I could not move. My hands, feet, and neck seemed paralyzed and I was not even able to shout. For a moment I thought I was dead, but as I tried to understand what was happening to me, I failed to find a logical explanation. After struggling to free myself for almost two hours, I cried out to God saying, "O Lord, if this is you, free me and I promise I will search for you." After this short prayer, I found I could move again. My whole worldview had collapsed in just one night. Now, how could I continue to actively support atheism at Bethlehem University? How could I explain what had happened to me? I got up, drank some water, and went back to bed. Later, I was afraid to say that God did not exist. I was even afraid to walk in dark places because my mysterious supernatural encounter had happened in the dark. In short, I was puzzled and needed answers, so I started searching for God.

In 1987, I began to study the Bible, but I was disturbed by what I discovered. I argued, "How can someone live on earth for fifty or sixty years and then be cast into hell by God for eternity? This is unfair." During this period, I was invited to attend a special "revival meeting" at the Alliance Church in Jerusalem, and consequently, I decided to follow Jesus Christ. I felt that God was speaking to me and asking me to give him my heart. I answered saying, "Lord, I don't have a problem giving you my heart, but I do have a problem giving you my mind." I knew that I was a sinner and that I needed to be saved, but I was not completely convinced of the justice of Christianity. However, I decided to take a step of faith; I told the Lord that I would give him my heart, but that I had to trust him to convince me intellectually.

During the same period of time, I had three dreams. In the first dream, I saw myself walking down a path full of ugly faces on both sides. I was following a man I did not know, holding onto his long cloak while many terrifying faces surrounded me. In the second dream, I was in a transparent glass box surrounded by the same ugly and terrifying faces, but the box prevented them from touching or hurting me. In the third and final dream, I was on the same path as in the first dream, with the same ugly faces, but this time I was not following the man wearing the cloak. Instead, he was holding me in his arms, and whenever I opened my eyes in my dream, I saw his face and this brought peace and tranquility to my heart. When I woke up God spoke to my heart, and the first thought that struck me was, "this is the difference between works and grace. If you want to follow me by your own efforts you will lose me, because you cannot keep holding onto my cloak by your own strength. If you are in Christ (in the box), then I will carry you." This is grace. These dreams were a turning point in my life. God became so personal to me. He won my heart and my mind and I accepted Jesus Christ as my Savior and Lord, knowing that he died on the cross in my place.

From that moment, I started experiencing significant changes in my life. This inner transformation touched not only my intellect, but also my behavior. I stopped many of my bad habits, such as smoking, gambling, and cursing, but unfortunately, I also lost many of my friends who did not approve of my new lifestyle. However, a few of my friends did accept the Lord. I started reading my Bible daily, and by the grace of God, learned about his just love. I decided to give him all of my life and started a Bible study at Bethlehem University where I used to promote atheism. The Bible shaped my understanding of God and my role in life. However, there were still difficult challenges ahead of me, for the Bible commanded me to love my enemies! If I accepted the authority of the Bible, then I should obey its commandment to love. The Bible says:

> You have heard that it was said, "Love your neighbor and hate your enemy." But I tell you: Love your enemies and pray for those who persecute you, that you may be sons of your Father in heaven. He causes his sun to rise on the evil and the good, and sends rain on the righteous and the unrighteous. If you love those who love you, what reward will you get? Are not even the tax collectors doing that? And if you greet only your brothers, what are you doing more than others? Do not even pagans do that? Be perfect, therefore, as your heavenly Father is perfect. (Matt 5:43–48 NIV)

LOVING MY ENEMY

It was nearly midnight when I closed up the office of the Alliance Church in Jerusalem, stuffed the stack of pamphlets I had just finished photocopying inside my jacket, and began an uneasy walk home. In the late 1980s, under a new Israeli law, if an Israeli soldier called out to a Palestinian and the Palestinian did not respond, the soldier could consider that person a political fanatic and shoot him. During that time, many Palestinians distributed political flyers challenging the authority of the Israeli government. As I neared the Damascus Gate, I saw three Israeli soldiers standing in the shadows, watching me. One soldier lifted a hand and crooked his finger commanding me to approach them. There was no one else in sight, and as

I approached the soldiers, my heart pounded and I began to pray. Without thinking, I rapidly unzipped my jacket, and just as quickly found three machine guns aimed at my head!

I stared at the soldiers. I had seen many soldiers who looked just like these men, mocking the students at Bethlehem University, forcing them to stay indoors during a sudden curfew that could last for weeks, allowing no possibility to work, buy food, or get medical attention. I looked at them and raised my hand to my chest. "I have a heart, here, that loves you," I told them. For a moment, the three soldiers stared at me, shocked. I was shocked, too! Slowly, they lowered their guns and we began to talk together. After twenty minutes, one soldier told me, "I wish that all Palestinians were like you." "No", I replied. "I wish that you were like me."

That incident helped me to reflect on how Christ had changed me. Only two years earlier, Christ's command in the Sermon on the Mount to love your enemies seemed impossible to me. And yet, there it was—unambiguous and unchanging. For me, love was an active decision, counter to the culture in which I lived—a culture where hatred of the other abounded, fuelled by the circumstances of daily life, the media, attitudes—all contributing to the alienation of both Israeli Jews and Palestinian Arabs. To overcome this alienation and hatred, I needed a profound change.

At first I tried, but failed, in my attempts to feel love. Israeli soldiers would stop Palestinians daily, at random, and ask for their identification cards, sometimes detaining them for hours. These experiences fueled my fear and anger. As I confessed my inability to love to God, I realized something significant. The radical love of Christ is not an emotion, but a decision. I decided to show love, however reluctantly, by sharing the gospel message with the soldiers on the street.

With new resolve, I began to carry tracts written in Hebrew and English with a quotation from Isaiah 53, and the words "Real Love" printed across the top. Every time a soldier stopped me, I handed him both my ID card and a tract. Because the quote came from the Hebrew Scriptures, the soldiers usually asked me about it before letting me go. After several months of this, I suddenly realized that my feelings toward the soldiers had changed. I was surprised. It was a process that I had been unaware of, but my former feelings were gone. I would pass the same way and see the same soldiers as before, but now I found myself praying, "Lord, let them stop me so I can share with them the love of Christ."

Opposition served as a reminder to me that I needed to decide daily whether or not I would choose to love. Sin distorts your mind and you can easily revert to the ways of human nature and respond with hate when treated badly. But really, our "love muscles" grow stronger as we obey God, and after some time we become more patient. We have more strength to love. Our hearts grow bigger, and we learn how to involve prayer in our love.

A recent incident challenged me again to demonstrate the love of God. I was invited to present an academic lecture at Lund University in Sweden. In the group of speakers were Muslims, Jews, and Christians, including several Jewish professors from Israeli universities. We visited a mosque, a church, and a synagogue. At the synagogue, I put on a skull cap and listened to three religious Jewish speakers, two men and one woman. For almost forty minutes they listed only negative aspects of Palestinians and spoke of how Palestinians persecute and torture Jews. Many statements were simply wrong. None of the speakers knew that there was a Palestinian in the audience, and when they concluded their lecture, invited questions and comments. I stood up and said, "I am a Palestinian Christian. I empathize with your pain, even though I have different convictions, and I am sorry that you had to go through so much pain. I just want to tell you that I love you." Then I sat down.

The speakers were confused and did not know how to respond. Later, one of the Jewish Israeli professors told me, "I am amazed by love in Christianity." I replied that love is also found in the Hebrew Scriptures. He responded saying, "But it is central in your faith." For me, this kind of love is not an excuse to abandon justice, but is a motive to pursue it with all of my heart. In fact, this is my reason for writing this book: to promote a biblical view of land that is rooted in biblical love, faithful to the Bible, and that seeks justice for both Palestinians and Israelis. Thus in the next chapter, I will interact with many brothers and sisters in Christ who continue to affirm that the current state of Israel is the fulfillment of prophecies.

two

Three Important Questions

PALESTINIANS AND ISRAELI JEWS live today in one land, yet they live as two distinct communities, each of which claims ownership of the same territory. How are we to understand the divine promise pertaining to the land? Did God promise the land exclusively to the Jewish people? Do the Palestinians have a right to live in the land or does God want them to leave?

Some claim that the Jewish people have a divinely endorsed, perpetual right of ownership to the land, while others claim that the promises referring to the land have been fulfilled in the New Testament.[1] Where is Christ in this debate? In this present time, does the land belong to Israel or to Christ?

Let us consider the theological argument that God gave the land to Israel.[2] There are three pertinent questions: (1) what are the borders of the land, (2) who is Israel, and (3) how did God give Israel the land? We will address these important questions. Then I will present my theological study of the Scriptures concerning the land in three time periods: before the time of Abraham, during the time from Abraham to Christ, and after the coming of Christ.

This brings us to a discussion of an important theological premise: God gave the land to Israel. Many Christians believe that modern Israel is

---

1. Further details are found in Loden et al., *Bible and the Land.*

2. This chapter is based on two articles that I have written: "Christ Is the Owner of Haaretz" and "Eschatology from a Palestinian Perspective." The first is published in English and the second in Arabic. See Katanacho, "Christ Is the Owner of Haaretz," 425–41; "Lahoot Akher al-Ayyam min Minthar Filsteeni," 106–16.

more theologically significant than other states. This belief might be embedded in dispensational theology which makes a crucial distinction between Israel and the church.[3] In fact, some see it as the essence of dispensationalism.[4] A brief summary of the development of dispensationalism will help clarify the roots of this belief.[5]

John Darby (1800–1882), the father of dispensationalism, made a clear distinction between Israel and the church, and established a strict dichotomy between two peoples.[6] He argued that Israel is an earthly people, promised a material and worldly kingdom, while the largely Gentile church is a spiritual people, promised a heavenly kingdom.[7] Darby's theology was popularized by the Scofield Reference Bible that first appeared in 1909, and more recently by the Ryrie Study Bible, especially its expanded edition, in 1994. While contemporary dispensationalists would disagree with many of the details of Darby's argument, they also assert the need to maintain a distinction between Israel and the church.[8] They see that many Old Testament promises made to ethnic Israel will be fulfilled in a future earthly kingdom, thus following the literal hermeneutics that Darby advocated.

In short, throughout its history, dispensationalism taught an earthly/heavenly dualism between Israel and the church, promoting two different programs in God's purposes, one for the church, and another for Israel. In Israel's program the land is deemed crucial. In the words of Lewis Chafer (1871–1952), the founder of Dallas Theological Seminary, "Israel can never be blessed apart from her land."[9] They see that many Old Testament promises made to ethnic Israel will be fulfilled in a future earthly kingdom, thus following the literal hermeneutics that Darby advocated. National Israel has a future role in her land because of her unconditional, divinely bestowed privileges and promises for her restored life on this earth.[10]

3. Sizer, "Dispensational Approaches," 142–71.

4. Ryrie, *Dispensationalism Today*, 47.

5. Some scholars argue that dispensationalism or its roots can be traced back to the early church. See Ehlert, *Bibliographic History*, 6. However, this claim is anachronistic and ignores some of the unprecedented claims of dispensationalism, e.g., the rapture theory that promotes two second comings, a secretive one followed by a public one.

6. Kreider, "Darby," 550.

7. Ibid.

8. Crutchfield, *Origins of Dispensationalism*, 205.

9. Chafer, *Systematic Theology*, 323.

10. See the doctrinal statement of Dallas Theological Seminary, article XX. Both classical and progressive dispensationalists on the faculty of Dallas subscribe to its statement

These dispensational beliefs gave theological support for the establishment of the state of Israel in 1948, and its preservation in the following decades. Popular writers like Hal Lindsey, Tim Lahaye, and John Hagee have influenced American public opinion regarding Israel in unprecedented ways. They have provided a prophetic lens for interpreting the whole world in light of the political events of the state of Israel. Its establishment became for many, the most important event since Christ's ascension.[11] Some televangelists further popularized this theology to teach that to stand against Israel in this earthly history is to stand against God.[12]

It is important, however, to assert that dispensationalists are not the only group who are interested in the future of ethnic Israel. Jewish and Christian Zionists as well as restorationists are also interested in the future of ethnic Israel.[13] Hornstra rightly distinguishes between restorationism and Zionism.[14] Both claim that God will restore the Jews to the Holy Land. However, they have several differences. First, restorationism is older than Christian Zionism. Its origin can be found in British Puritanism roughly around 1600. Second, restorationists are interested in evangelizing the Jews but were passive in 1948. They are less political. On the other hand, many Christian Zionists continue to support the State of Israel based on ideological and even religious convictions. Their perception of the State of Israel is not only based on a hermeneutical and a theological or eschatological understanding but also on the history of the relationship between Christians and Jews as well as on interpreting the modern history of the Middle East as part of salvation history. Third, restorationists are different from Christian Zionists for although they subscribe to both literalism and Jewish restoration, they are not necessarily dispensationalists. In fact, restorationists existed long before dispensationalism. Nevertheless, the questions related to Israel's identity, relationship to God and land are relevant to restorationists, dispensationalists, and Christian Zionists, although admittedly in different ways.

---

of faith. Dallas Theological Seminary, "Article XX–The Second Coming of Christ," n.p.

11. Falwell, "Twenty-First Century," 10–11.

12. Falwell, *Listen, America!*, 215.

13. It is important to point out that Zionism has many forms. Political Zionism is different from religious Zionism. Further, Jewish Zionism and Christian Zionism are extremely different in their origin and are also different in their claims.

14. Hornstra, "Christian Zionism among Evangelicals in the Federal Republic of Germany"; Hornstra, "Western Restorationists and Christian Zionism," 131–48. Please note that the names Willem and Wilrens refer to the same person.

At the cost of oversimplification, many Western Christians assume today that God gave Israel the land, an assumption that gives religious support to the West's political stance on the Middle East. But this assumption requires further probing: (1) what do we mean by "the land" or ha'aretz, (2) who is Israel, and (3) how did God give the land to Israel?[15]

What Are the Borders of the Land of Israel?

Defining modern Israel's borders based on the Bible is difficult because the Bible gives a number of different borders. In the Pentateuch alone we encounter at least three different borders (Gen 15:18–20, Num 34:1–12, and Deut 11:24, cf. Josh 1:3, 13–19). Genesis 15:18 states that the land is "from the river of Egypt to the great river, the Euphrates." The Euphrates begins in Turkey and flows through Syria and Iraq before entering the Persian Gulf. Furthermore, if we follow in the footsteps of several significant commentators who claim that the "river of Egypt" is the Nile, then we are referring to a territory that extends from Egypt to Iraq.[16] If these borders are literally applied today, then Genesis 15:18 is referring to a land that includes parts of Egypt, Lebanon, most of Syria, Jordan, Palestine, Iraq, Kuwait, and parts of Saudi Arabia.[17]

On the other hand, the book of Deuteronomy says, "Your territory will extend from the desert to Lebanon and from the Euphrates River to the western sea." Eugene Merrill comments on this verse, saying that the borders are from the Negev to Lebanon and from the Euphrates to the Mediterranean Sea.[18] The book of Joshua describes how these lands were distributed among the different tribes. The borders in Deuteronomy and in Joshua are different from the ones in Genesis 15:18. The map titled "The Tribes of Israel in the Land" should help us to visualize the pertinent borders.

15. As Janzen clarifies, "The two common English designations 'Promised Land' and 'Holy Land,' though correctly expressing central theological concerns, are not characteristic of the Old Testament." Janzen, "Land," 144. Thus I prefer to use the word "the land" even though it has many limitations. At least it is not loaded theologically and it is not anachronistic. The Hebrew word Ha'aretz simply means the land. It could refer to a specific piece of land or to the whole earth.

16. It is not clear whether the river of Egypt refers to Wadi el Arish or the Nile. However, the latter is more probable. For further details, see the comments on Genesis 15:18 in Wenham, *Genesis 1–15*. See also Spence-Jones, *Genesis*.

17. Sizer, *Zion's Christian Soldiers?*, 78.

18. See the comments on Deut 11:24 in Merrill, *Deuteronomy*.

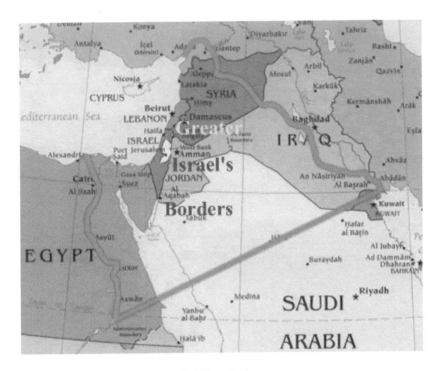

From the Nile to the Euphrates

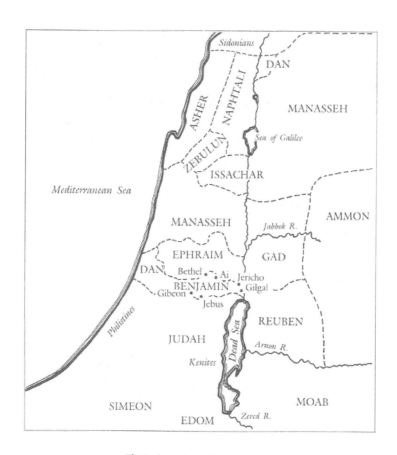

The Tribes of Israel in the Land

The land was allotted to nine and a half tribes, since two and a half tribes settled in Transjordan. The book of Numbers describes yet another border. Numbers 34:3–12 says,

> Your southern side will include some of the Desert of Zin along the border of Edom. On the east, your southern boundary will start from the end of the Salt Sea, cross south of Scorpion Pass, continue on to Zin and go south of Kadesh Barnea. Then it will go to Hazar Addar and over to Azmon, where it will turn, join the Wadi of Egypt and end at the Sea. Your western boundary will be the coast of the Great Sea. This will be your boundary on the west. For your northern boundary, run a line from the Great Sea to Mount Hor and from Mount Hor to Lebo Hamath. Then the boundary will go to Zedad, continue to Ziphron and end at Hazar Enan. This will be your boundary on the north. For your eastern boundary, run a line from Hazar Enan to Shepham. The boundary will go down from Shepham to Riblah on the east side of Ain and continue along the slopes east of the Sea of Kinnereth. Then the boundary will go down along the Jordan and end at the Salt Sea. This will be your land, with its boundaries on every side.

The northern and eastern boundaries are strikingly different from those found in Genesis 15:18 or Deuteronomy 11:24. Recognizing these territorial differences, Kallai suggests three possibilities, namely: the land of the patriarchs (Gen 15:18), the land of Canaan (Num 34:1–12; cf. Num 34:2, 29), and the land of Israel (Deut 11:24).[19] He argues that the land of the patriarchs, i.e., the land between Egypt and Mesopotamia, including the nomadic desert fringe, is the core of the covenantal land; the land of Canaan is the promised land; and the land of Israel is the realization of this promise. The following map visually demonstrates the territorial differences between the land of Canaan and the land of Israel.

The land of Canaan (surrounded by a dark black line) includes parts of modern Lebanon and Syria, while the land of Israel (covered by horizontal lines) has territory in Transjordan outside the land of Canaan. It includes a bigger part of modern Jordan. Finally, we observe lands with blank spaces indicating lands not occupied by the ancient Israelites even though some of them were allotted to certain tribes.

---

19. Kallai, "Patriarchal Boundaries, Canaan and the Land of Israel," 70.

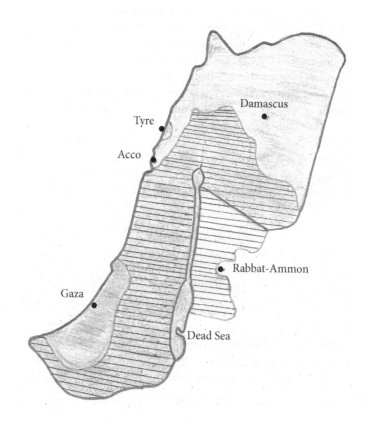

The Land of Canaan and the Land of Israel

Jeffrey Townsend had suggested earlier that there are general descriptions of the land (Gen 15:18; Ex 23:31; Num 13:21; Deut 11:24; 1 Kgs 8:65; 2 Kgs 14:25) and specific descriptions (Num 34:1–12; Josh 15:1–12; Ezek 47:15–20).[20] He adds that these two options are not contradictory because the wider borders are only general and variable approximations. There is a distinction between the land of the Israelites' residence and the land where they exercise sovereignty. Moshe Weinfeld finds yet another explanation for these territorial differences based on the documentary hypothesis that the final text comes from four independent literary sources.[21] He simply believes that there are different borders from different literary sources.

However, none of these explanations is satisfactory. Kallai lacks sufficient textual support for his tripartite division of the land—the land of the patriarchs, the land of Canaan, and the land of Israel. Townsend downplays the huge territorial differences, especially the northern and eastern dimensions. Weinfeld ignores the present textus receptus, underestimating the intelligentsia of ancient Israel. How did the Israelites justify having three different, and paradoxically contradictory, borders in the final form of the biblical text? Why did they not say anything about it? In short, it is important to assert that these scholars have rightly highlighted the territorial diversity in the Old Testament, challenging any notion of fixed borders. Their assertion that there are different borders can be confirmed by other Old Testament writings. The book of Ezekiel (Ezek 47:17–18), for example, refers to northern borders that are near Damascus, and eastern boundaries that run along the Jordan River valley to the Dead Sea. The aforementioned authors are right in pointing out different borders but they have not paid sufficient attention to the theological framework, namely, God's redemptive plan for the whole world—the whole earth. Later, we will elaborate on the importance of not having fixed borders, but first, let us consider the second question: who is Israel?

---

20. Townsend, "Fulfillment of the Land Promise," 320–37.

21. The German scholar Julius Wellhausen (1844–1918) advocated this hypothesis. He believed that the Pentateuch comes from four independent literary sources that are identified as J (Yahwist), E (Elohist), D (Deuteronomist), and P (Priestly). For further details, consult Weinfeld, *Promise of the Land*, 52–75.

WHO IS ISRAEL?

As we can see in the works of Kallai, Townsend, and Weinfeld, formulating clear criteria for the content and indicators of Israel's identity is extremely difficult. This is even more difficult when the term "Israel" is used, as do some prominent Christians, to refer to both the modern state of Israel and biblical Israel. Such equivocality is not only anachronistic but also overlooks important complexities, sacrificing Israel's diachronic meanings for the sake of a fixed synchronic understanding of Israel as a nation. To simplify, equating the modern state of Israel to biblical Israel is a common error among many dispensationalists. The following examples should illustrate this point.[22] First, John Walvoord described the return of millions of Jews to *their ancient land*, as the *restoration* of national Israel in 1948, and its expansion in 1967 as fulfillment of prophecy.[23] In his opinion, the establishment of the state of Israel is one of the most remarkable prophetic fulfillments since the destruction of Jerusalem in AD 70.[24] Further, the preservation of Israel since its establishment is a clear sign of divine blessing.[25] Second, on November 1, 1977, the *New York Times* ran a full-page ad headed "Evangelicals' Concern for Israel," signed by many influential Evangelicals, including Hudson Amerding, W. A. Criswell, John Walvoord, and Kenneth Kantzer. It reads (in part):

> We the undersigned evangelical Christians affirm our belief in the right of Israel to exist . . . we, along, with most evangelicals, understand the Jewish homeland generally to include the territory west of the Jordan River. . . . We would view with grave concern any effort to carve out of the historic Jewish homeland another nation or political entity, particularly one which would be governed by terrorists. . . . The time has come for Evangelical Christians to affirm their belief in Biblical prophecy and Israel's Divine Right to the Land by speaking now. [26]

22. A long list of illustrations can be found in the impressive work of Boyer, *When Time Shall Be No More*, 80–112.

23. Walvoord was the president of Dallas Theological Seminary from 1952–1986. Walvoord, *Major Bible Prophecies*, 70. It is important to note that the restoration of "Israel" is different from their salvation. The former includes the idea of Israel being replanted in her land and given a unique role and mission to the nations. They will have a prominent role among the nations.

24. Ibid., 7, 71–72, 319.

25. Walvoord, "Amazing Rise of Israel," 22.

26. This quotation can be found in Merkley, *Christian Attitudes*, 167–68.

Third, on the website of the International Christian Embassy Jerusalem, the executive director Malcolm Hedding, affirmed in 2010 that the "Jewish people" have the right to return to their homeland on scriptural grounds and "Israel's re-emergence on the world's scene, in fulfillment of God's promises to her, indicate that other biblically predicted events will follow."[27] These examples assume continuity between biblical Israel and the modern state of Israel. But there are better arguments for the multiple meanings of "Israel" in both Testaments.

Israel in the Old Testament

As Old Testament scholar Gerhard von Rad has shown, we find a plurality of meanings already in the Old Testament.[28] During the lifetime of Jacob, "Israel" denoted Jacob (Gen 32:28), his children (Gen 34:7), and his tribe (Gen 47:27; 49:28).

> Your name will no longer be Jacob, but **Israel**, because you have struggled with God and with men and have overcome.
> (Gen 32:28)[29]

> Now Jacob's sons had come in from the fields as soon as they heard what had happened. They were filled with grief and fury, because Shechem had done a disgraceful thing in **Israel** by lying with Jacob's daughter—a thing that should not be done.
> (Gen 34:7)

> Now the **Israelites** settled in Egypt in the region of Goshen. They acquired property there and were fruitful and increased greatly in number.
> (Gen 47:27)

During the lifetime of Moses, "Israel" referred to the descendants of Jacob's tribe. Exodus 1:7 says, "But the Israelites were fruitful and multiplied greatly and became exceedingly numerous, so that the land was filled with them." Joshua 22:1–11 refers to Jacob's descendants excluding the Reubenites, the Gadites, and the half-tribe of Manasseh. The text reads:

27. Hedding, "Christian Zionism 101," n.p.

28. Von Rad, "Israel, Judah, and Hebrews in the Old Testament," 356–58.

29. All the bold fonts in the biblical texts are added. They are not part of the original text unless stated otherwise.

> When they came to Geliloth near the Jordan in the land of Canaan, the Reubenites, the Gadites and the half-tribe of Manasseh built an imposing altar there by the Jordan. And when the **Israelites** heard that they had built the altar on the border of Canaan at Geliloth near the Jordan on the **Israelite** side, the whole assembly of **Israel** gathered at Shiloh to go to war against them.

In Judges 20:35, the term "Israel" denotes Jacob's descendants excluding Benjamin. It says, "The Lord defeated Benjamin before Israel, and on that day the Israelites struck down 25,100 Benjamites, all armed with swords." During the period of the united kingdom of Israel, and before the fall of Samaria, the term "Israel" may exclude the men of Judah (1 Sam 17:52; 18:16), or may represent Absalom's men who rebelled against David (2 Sam 17:24), or may stand for the northern kingdom.

> Then the men of **Israel** and Judah surged forward with a shout and pursued the Philistines to the entrance of Gathand to the gates of Ekron. Their dead were strewn along the Shaaraim road to Gath and Ekron. (1 Sam 17:52)

> But all **Israel** and Judah loved David, because he led them in their campaigns. (1 Sam 18:16)

> David went to Mahanaim, and Absalom crossed the Jordan with all the men of **Israel.** (2 Sam 17:24)

These verses *inter alia* demonstrate that the term "Israel" does not necessarily include Judah. Also, 2 Samuel 17:24 shows that the phrase "all the men of Israel" excludes David and his men.

After the fall of the northern kingdom, many prophets like Isaiah, Jeremiah, and Ezekiel used the term "Israel" to refer to all the followers of Yahweh. Watts illustrates this point arguing that "Israel" in certain parts of Isaiah denotes all the followers of Yahweh. Commenting on Isaiah 56:1–8, he says,

> The foreigners are described in four ways: they join themselves to Yahweh, that is, they become proselytes; they minister to him, that is, they are prepared to perform services in the Temple (cf. 66:21); they love the name of Yahweh, that is, they are devoted to him beyond the acts of worship themselves; and they become his servants (cf. 54:17c). This group includes all who keep Sabbath holy and who hold fast his covenant. This implies a return to the original understanding of Israel as a worshiping and covenanting congregation, composed of persons who swore fealty to Yahweh

in covenant ceremonies (cf. Ex 19:1—20:21; Deuteronomy; Josh 24). . . . Commitment and acceptance of responsibility are more important than the birthright; cf. the story of Esau and Jacob in Gen 25:29–34. The Vision shows that Israel/Jacob also despised his birthright. Now others, more worthy, are invited to enter into it. . . . Yahweh continues his efforts to gain Jewish devotees who will do his will, keep his covenant, and love his name (cf. Paul's emphasis in Rom 9–11, which quotes liberally from Isaiah). But he does not limit himself to those who are "Israel according to the flesh."[30]

Spence-Jones agrees with Watts's main argument. He comments on Isaiah 56:8 saying,

[The Lord] has pledged himself to bring back Israel from captivity, and to gather together Israel's outcasts from all regions (ch. 11:11; 27:12–13; 43:5–6, etc.). This same Lord now promises something further: "He will gather others also to Israel, besides his own gathered ones." Introduced with such emphasis and formality, this was probably, when delivered, a new revelation. In the present arrangement of the prophecies, however, it announces no novelty. The addition of Gentile members to the Israelite community has been declared frequently. (see ch. 44:5; 55:5, etc.)[31]

During the period of Ezra and Nehemiah, however, this inclusive approach faced several challenges, and might wrongly be defined as the purity of lineage. Ezra 9:2 says that the "holy race" has mingled with other nations. It is unfortunate that some English translations still use the word "race" which has the twentieth-century perception of differentiating groups of people according to biological and physical features, and associating these with intellectual and behavioral traits. The adjective "holy" shows that the term "race" has nothing to do with racial prejudice. Instead, it is "a question of the living relationship between the LORD and his people, and not of who one's ancestors might be."[32] The text in Ezra is not interested in biological differences or DNA, but in following the Lord. Ezra considers the mingling with other nations as unfaithfulness. As the people of Israel mingled with other nations, they also worshipped their gods. Thus, they were unfaithful to Yahweh, guilty before God, as they broke his commandment not to bow

---

30. Watts, *Isaiah 34–66*; Isa 56:1–8.

31. Spence-Jones, *Isaiah*; Isa 56:8.

32. Fensham, *Books of Ezra and Nehemiah*, 125.

down to other gods. In short, the Old Testament data demonstrates the accuracy of von Rad's claim that there are many meanings for the word "Israel" in the Old Testament.

Israel in the New Testament

The New Testament also includes a plurality of meanings. "Israel" might designate God's people who are led by a shepherd king from Bethlehem. Matthew 2:6 says, "But you, Bethlehem, in the land of Judah, are by no means least among the rulers of Judah; for out of you will come a ruler who will be the shepherd of my people Israel." Further, the term "Israel" might refer to a land. Matthew says, "Get up [Joseph], take the child and his mother and go to the land of Israel, for those who were trying to take the child's life are dead" (Matt 2:20). In Matthew, "Israel" is the twelve tribes judged by the twelve apostles (Matt 19:28), while in Acts 2:22, "Israel" is associated with the Jews who were in Jerusalem.

The apostle Paul has a unique contribution to make since he uses the term "Israel" in different ways. The apostle Paul makes the following argument in Romans 9:3–8:

> For I could wish that I myself were cursed and cut off from Christ for the sake of my brothers, those of my own race, the people of Israel. Theirs is the adoption as sons; theirs the divine glory, the covenants, the receiving of the law, the temple worship and the promises. Theirs are the patriarchs, and from them is traced the human ancestry of Christ, who is God over all, forever praised! Amen. It is not as though God's word had failed. For not all who are descended from Israel are Israel. Nor because they are his descendants are they all Abraham's children. On the contrary, "It is through Isaac that your offspring will be reckoned." In other words, it is not the natural children who are God's children, but it is the children of the promise who are regarded as Abraham's offspring.

Paul calls the people of Israel "my own race." The Greek origin of the word "race" is "*sun-genes.*" It could mean "a person who is related by blood" or, "a person who is a fellow citizen." The apostle Peter uses a closely related word "genes" which is translated as "race" in the Revised Standard Version. The context of the first epistle of Peter makes it absolutely clear that the intended "race" is related to all those who believe in Jesus Christ. The term is not used in a biological sense. However, many people perceive the idea of "race" as an ethnic group related by genealogy and similar biological and genetic traits, or physical characteristics. A closer look at Paul's argument reveals that he does not see DNA as the defining factor of the term "Israel." In fact Paul, in Romans 9, argues that "not all who are descended from Israel are Israel" (Rom 9:6). In other words, Paul gives some criteria that help us to define "Israel." His perception of the people of Israel is related to their relationship to God, not to their biological ancestry. The Tyndale Concise Bible Commentary states that the "Israel spoken of in the Old Testament promises is not identical with the natural and physical descendants of Jacob."[33] Physical descent is simply not enough, for Ishmael, too, was a son of Abraham. Belonging to Israel is not related to biology but to faith.

The Term "Hebrew" in the Bible

We have seen so far that the term "Israel" has many meanings in the Bible. It is equally important to clarify some of the differences between the terms "Israel," "Hebrew," and "Jew." Biblically, the term "Israel" has many meanings and is distinct from the term "Hebrew," or "Jew." A person could be a Hebrew, but not Jewish or Israelite—for example, Abraham. The word "Hebrew" occurs about 37 times in the Old Testament and 12 times in the New Testament. It refers to a language or to a non-exclusive ethnic group, and it could also refer to a social class such as strangers or foreigners. Most likely, its meaning must allow a connection to Eber (Gen 10:24) and/or to Abraham. As a result, the term "Hebrew" broadens the identity of those who are called Hebrews beyond the children of Jacob and their descendants, encouraging us to see "Hebrew" as a fluid term, not a rigid term. This fluidity helps us to understand that the Old Testament texts (1) call Abram a Hebrew (Gen 14:13); (2) call the land from which Joseph was taken as the land of the Hebrews, even though the children of Jacob were around 70 people (Gen 40:15, 46:26); (3) describe the existence of a group called Hebrews, even though they were not counted with all the men of Israel (1 Sam 14:21–22); and at the same time (4) define Jonah's identity as Hebrew (Jonah 1:9). In simple words, Abraham was a Hebrew, but not an Israelite or a Jew.

Furthermore, one could be a member of Israel and a Hebrew without being Jewish—for example, the prophet Samuel. He lived at a time in which

33. Hughes and Laney, *Tyndale Concise Bible Commentary*, 537; Rom 9:6–13.

the referent "Jew" was not yet coined. One could be Jewish but not an Is-raelite or Hebrew—for example, Antiochus the Macedonian king (2 Mac 9:17). A person could be brought into the household of Israel and could become Jewish, but not a Hebrew or a descendant of Jacob—for example, Achior the Ammonite (Judith 14:10). In other words, the terms "Israel," "Jew," and "Hebrew" are not identical, and perhaps it is unwise to assume that the promises given to the Hebrews are transferred to the Israelites, and later to the Jews, without providing sufficient biblical support. It will be helpful, then, to study the term "Jew" in the Bible.

The Term "Jew" in the Old Testament

The term "Jew" occurs dozens of times in the Old Testament, frequently in the book of Esther. The term "Jew," however, was used for the first time in 2 Kings 16:6, and thus it is arguably a newer term than "Hebrew" or "Israel." It is not found in the Pentateuch, (the first five books of the Bible), even though the word Judah is used. At first, the term "Jew" was used to denote the inhabitants of Judah and their children. Later, this definition was broadened as more followers of Yahweh started coming to Jerusalem to worship Yahweh (2 Chronicles 30). At that time, the inhabitants of the southern kingdom developed an inclusive attitude, centered on their re-ligious identity. By the time of Jeremiah, the term "Jew" included groups living in Moab, Ammon, Edom, and those exiled to Babylonia (Jer 40:11; 52:28–30). By the time of Esther, it could have been radically redefined in certain circles to denote anyone, regardless of ethnicity, who joined the people of Yahweh and shared their faith. The book of Esther uses a *Hithpaʿel* Hebrew form (מתיהדים) of the word "Jew" to state that many nations be-came Jews during the time of Esther. It reads, "In every province and in every city, wherever the edict of the king went, there was joy and gladness among the Jews, with feasting and celebrating. And many people of other nationalities became Jews because fear of the Jews had seized them" (Esth 8:17). This is amazing for the original Hebrew text states that many nations became Jews. The Hebrew text uses the word "Jew" as a verb instead of a noun. Bush points out that the Hebrew text should be translated as "many of the peoples of the Land became Jews." The land refers to the land of Palestine, and the new converts are its non-Jewish population.[34]

34. Bush, *Ruth, Esther*; Esth 8:17.

The Term "Jew" in the New Testament

Moreover, the word "Jew" in the New Testament occurs hundreds of times with a spectrum of nuances, even within one epistle or book. For example, it could mean the Jews who did not accept the resurrection of Christ (Matt 28:15); or devout followers of Judaism from many nations (Acts 2:5); or a group who belonged to a certain ethnos (Acts 10:22). It could also mean Jewish followers of Christ. Paul, for example, describes himself as a Jew who believes in Jesus Christ (Acts 22:3–21). Other Christians use the word "Jew" to refer to themselves. The following three references are interesting:

> A man is not a Jew if he is only one outwardly, nor is circumcision merely outward and physical. No, a man is a Jew if he is one inwardly; and circumcision is circumcision of the heart, by the Spirit, not by the written code. Such a man's praise is not from men, but from God. (Rom 2:28–29)

> I know your afflictions and your poverty—yet you are rich! I know the slander of those who say they are Jews and are not, but are a synagogue of Satan. (Rev 2:9)

> I will make those who are of the synagogue of Satan, who claim to be Jews though they are not, but are liars—I will make them come and fall down at your feet and acknowledge that I have loved you. (Rev 3:9)

The first text reveals that there are those who seem Jewish outwardly, but are not considered Jews in the eyes of God who looks at our hearts. Consequently, the term "Jew" gains a spiritual component discerned by God and the question shifts from who is a Jew to, what makes a person a true Jew. James Dunn, in the Word Biblical Commentary, points out that Paul is critiquing those who emphasize outward or visible circumcision and physical kinship, for a true Jew is the one whom God praises.[35] Notice that the word Jew is derived from the word Yehuda which is associated with the one who is praised by God. Perhaps Jewishness should not be measured by visible or physical traits, or even rituals. It is something inward, related to the heart, and associated with the Spirit of God. This perception of Jewishness embodies the eschatological hope that the Holy Spirit will work in the hearts of both Gentiles and Jews. This hope was initiated in the ministry, death, and resurrection of Christ as he came to bring salvation

---

35. Dunn, *Romans 1–8*; Rom 2:28–29.

to all, Jew and Gentile. Therefore, "the eschatological Jew is Gentile as well as Jew!"[36] It seems that these eschatological Jews are the followers of Jesus Christ who come from both Gentile and Jewish backgrounds. The second text sounds offensive, especially to Jews. However, it is important to point out that the term "Jew" is used positively. According to this text, those who call themselves Jews and oppose the church of Christ are not worthy of being called Jews for they oppose Christ, who is the ultimate fulfillment of the Scriptures. Consequently, they are allies with the enemy of God. The third text confirms that the term "Jew" is reserved for those who do not oppose the body of the Messiah. The Jews who oppose the Jewish and Gentile followers of Jesus will "grovel before the feet of this (largely Gentile) Christian community."[37]

In summary, the distinctions between "Israel," "Hebrew," and "Jew" are important, but we are still left with the conundrum of Israel's identity. How can we understand what determines Israel's ethnicity? What makes a person a member of Israel? Is it lineage, religion, geography, culture, a combination of these elements, or something else? Let us continue our study of Israel's identity by considering intermarriages.

Intermarriage

To explore this question further, a look at Old Testament marriage customs and practices may be helpful. Although the descendants of Jacob preferred tribal intermarriage, they were not a closed group. In fact, we have several male descendants of Jacob who married foreigners. Judah married a Canaanite wife (Gen 38:2; 1 Chron 2:3). Joseph married an Egyptian (Gen 41:45). Simeon married a Canaanite (Gen 46:10). Moses married a Midianite (Exod 2:21–22). Solomon married many foreign wives. The Bible says, "King Solomon, however, loved many foreign women besides Pharaoh's daughter—Moabites, Ammonites, Edomites, Sidonians and Hittites. . . . He had seven hundred wives of royal birth and three hundred concubines" (1 Kgs 11:1–3). These intermarriages were not limited to the well-known, for we are told in the book of Judges that many of the descendants of Jacob had foreign wives. The Bible says, "The Israelites lived among the Canaanites, Hittites, Amorites, Perizzites, Hivites and Jebusites. They took their daughters in marriage and gave their own daughters to their sons, and

36. Ibid.

37. Aune, *Revelation 1–5*; Rev 3:9.

served their gods" (Judg 3:5–6). Consequently, they became one people with these nations (Gen 34:16). Both Israelite men and women had foreign spouses. Are their children full members of Israel? Did these spouses offer any cultural contributions to Israel's identity?

Besides the men who married foreign women, there are female descendants of Jacob who married foreign men. Shelomith, the daughter of Dibri the Danite married an Egyptian (Lev 24:10–12). A Nephtalite woman married a Phoenician man, giving birth to Hiram (1 Kgs 7:13–14), a prominent biblical figure known for his contribution to the building of the first temple during Solomon's era. Hiram's mother was an Israelite from the tribe of Naphtali while his father was a man of Tyre.

Adoption and Bearing the Father's Name

To further complicate the issue, there are children who belonged to a certain lineage, but they were partially foreign to it. This was common among several ancient Near Eastern peoples.[38] However, it acquired different nuances in the Bible. We see it not only in the story of Abraham and his son Ishmael (Genesis 16), but also in the story of Judah who asked his second son to produce a child for his dead brother—an offspring from the sperm of the living brother, but legally belonging to the dead brother (Gen 38:8–9). This concept of sonship or of "legal belonging" can also be seen in Ex 21:3–4, where a fellow Israelite marries a bondwoman who bears children who belong to the household of the master (cf. Deut 15:12; Jer 34:9, 14).[39] It also extended to foreign slaves. When a foreign slave married an Israelite woman, their children belonged to the household of her father and bore his name.[40] In the genealogy of Judah we read: "Sheshan had no sons—only daughters. He had an Egyptian servant named Jarha. Sheshan gave his daughter in marriage to his servant Jarha, and she bore him Attai (1 Chr 2:34–35). In other words, Sheshan was continuing his line through his Egyptian servant. Commenting on 1 Chron 2:34–35, Jamieson et al say:

> The adoption and marriage of a foreign slave in the family where
> he is serving, is far from being a rare or extraordinary occurrence
> in Eastern countries. It is thought, however, by some to have been

38. Some examples could be seen in Hammurabi's Code § 146, or Nuzi or Neo-Assyrian texts. For further details, see Hamilton, *Book of Genesis*, 444–45.

39. Sarna, *Exodus*, 119.

40. Japhet, *I & II Chronicles*, 84.

a connection not sanctioned by the law of Moses [Michaelis]. But this is not a well-founded objection, as the history of the Jews furnishes not a few examples of foreign proselytes in the same manner obtaining an inheritance in Israel; and doubtless Jarha had previously embraced the Jewish faith in place of the grovelling idolatries of his native Egypt. In such a case, therefore, there could be no legal difficulty. Being a foreign slave, he had no inheritance in a different tribe to injure by this connection; while his marriage with Sheshan's daughter led to his adoption into the tribe of Judah, as well as his becoming heir of the family property.[41]

In short, borrowing Ezra's language, we can see that the "holy seed" has mingled with many nations (Ezra 9:2) and many cannot prove a pure lineage (Ezra 2:59; Neh 7:61, 64). If difficult then, how could we trace the ancestral relationship of the descendants of Jacob today? Would we define a member of Israel patrilineally, matrilineally or through both father's and mother's lineage? Would we look for purity of the bloodline, or would one drop of the blood of Jacob's descendants be sufficient to recognize a person as a member of Israel? What about the foreigners who joined the household of Israel? Would Ruth, the great grandmother of Jesus, and her descendants receive the promises; Ruth whose grandchild David, became one of Israel's greatest leaders? And lest one think that Ruth is an exception, consider Rahab (Josh 6:25) or the thirty-two thousand Midianite virgins (Num 31:35). These virgins became mothers in Israel.[42] Perhaps Israel's DNA is not the determining factor in deciding who inherits the land. We should seriously contemplate the claim that God can raise up children of Abraham out of stones (Matt 3:9; cf. John 8:37–39). Having a Gentile-free lineage does not make one a true Israelite. Otherwise the identity of Jesus, himself, would be questioned; he had several Gentile great grandmothers (cf. Matthew 1) and did not have a Jewish biological father. Moreover, would Jesus, who had a Jewish mother without a Jewish father, be considered a full member of Israel with full rights? In the final analysis, could it be that not all those who claim a physical connection with Jacob are true Israelites (cf. Rom 9:6)? It is fitting now to address our third question.

41. Jamieson et al., *Commentary, Critical and Explanatory*; 1 Chron 2:35.
42. Allen, "Numbers," 971.

How Did God Give Israel the Land?

Some Christians argue that the state of Israel is the fulfillment of biblical prophecies. They claim that God gave the land to the people of Israel. But what about the many biblical passages that require Israel to obey God as a condition to dwell or stay in the land and replace the wicked peoples who provoked his holy anger (cf. Deut 28:58–68, 30:15–20, Josh 23:12–16, or Ezek 33:21–29)?

> If you do not carefully follow all the words of this law, which are written in this book, and do not revere this glorious and awesome name—the Lord your God . . . you will be uprooted from the land you are entering to possess. (Deut 28:58–63)

> But if your heart turns away and you are not obedient, and if you are drawn away to bow down to other gods and worship them, I declare to you this day that you will certainly be destroyed. You will not live long in the land you are crossing the Jordan to enter and possess. (Deut 30:17–18)

> But just as every good promise of the LORD your God has come true, so the LORD will bring on you all the evil he has threatened, until he has destroyed you from this good land he has given you. If you violate the covenant of the LORD your God, which he commanded you, and go and serve other gods and bow down to them, the LORD's anger will burn against you, and you will quickly perish from the good land he has given you. (Josh 23:15–16)

The text in Ezekiel requires extra attention because several scholars and televangelists use it as proof that the modern state of Israel is the fulfillment of prophecy. Hughes and Laney, for example, say,

> The vision of the dry bones illustrated how the restoration of the nation (Ezek 36:24) will be accomplished. There were two stages in the resurrection of the dry bones (Ezek 37:7–10). As Ezekiel prophesied over the bones, they came together and formed human beings, but without the breath of life. Ezekiel prophesied again and "breath" came into them and they came to life (Ezek 37:9–10). In the interpretation of the vision it was revealed that Israel would first be brought to national life and restored to the land (Ezek 37:12), and then the Lord would give the nation spiritual life (Ezek 37:14). The first stage may have taken place on May 14, 1948,

when Israel once again became a nation after a two thousand-year eclipse.[43]

Hughes and Laney believe that possessing the land precedes the spiritual revival among the Israelites. Daniel Juster, a Messianic Jew, accepts the aforementioned explanation and extends it to illustrate the development within the Jewish Messianic community in the state of Israel, a community that is at the heart of the proper interpretation of the dry bones vision.[44] However, these approaches fail to pay enough attention to the literary and theological aspects of the book of Ezekiel.[45] Indeed, more responsible interpretations affirm the importance of Ezekiel's literary units and its holistic message.[46] The literary and theological message of Ezekiel 36 is related to Ezekiel 33–37, as affirmed by Leslie Allen.[47] In fact, chapter 33 should be considered an introduction to this literary unit, chapters 33–37.[48] Cooper accepts this assertion, stating that the book of Ezekiel is not a random collection of messages, and chapters 33–37 should be read together.[49] Taking this literary reality into consideration challenges a Christian Zionist interpretation of the dry bones vision simply because of the explicit language used in Ezekiel 33. It addresses the issue of land, inheritance, and Abraham saying,

> Then the word of the Lord came to me: "Son of man, the people living in those ruins in the land of Israel are saying, 'Abraham was only one man, yet he possessed the land. But we are many; surely the land has been given to us as our possession.' Therefore say to them, 'This is what the Sovereign Lord says: Since you eat meat with the blood still in it and look to your idols and shed blood, should you then possess the land? You rely on your sword, you do detestable things, and each of you defiles his neighbor's wife. Should you then possess the land?'" (Ezek 33:23–26)

We encounter in this text two theological schools of thought caught up in a debate. The first group, the non-exiled Judeans, argue that their

43. Hughes and Laney, *Tyndale Concise Bible Commentary*; Ezek 36:16—37:14.

44. Juster, "Dry Bones and Israel's Restoration," n.p.

45. A good example of a theological reading from a Jewish perspective is the work of Ganzel, "Descriptions of the Restoration of Israel in Ezekiel," 197–211.

46. For further details, see Strong, "Egypt's Shameful Death," 475–504.

47. Allen, *Ezekiel 20–48*, xxiii.

48. Ibid.

49. Cooper, *Ezekiel*; Ezek 33:1—48:35.

presence in the land is a sign of God's providential favor. They are pioneers like Abraham. They are the first fruit of the anticipated blessings and restoration. They are "religious pioneers, typologically reliving, not the occupation achieved by Israel under Joshua, but Abraham's earlier occupation (Gen 15:7, 8; Exod 6:8)."[50] This group focused on promise and inheritance. However, their theology is deficient because they separate theology from ethics and the fulfillment of the Abrahamic promise from morality. The second group, represented by Ezekiel, responds to their argument affirming that inheriting the land cannot be divorced from obedience to Yahweh and fidelity to his covenant. The first group thought that by claiming the fatherhood of Abraham they received free privileges. John the Baptist responded to a similar theology saying, "Do not think you can say to yourselves, 'We have Abraham as our father.' I tell you that out of these stones God can raise up children for Abraham. The ax is already at the root of the trees, and every tree that does not produce good fruit will be cut down and thrown into the fire" (Matt 3:9–10). Thus, Ezekiel argues that the disobedient will surely not inherit the land.

Consequently, it would be better to adopt Wright's interpretation arguing that the resurrection of the Messiah embodies the resurrection of Israel and fulfills the vision of Ezekiel.[51] He rightly relates the dry bones vision to the literary context. It is important to observe that Ezekiel lived hundreds of years after David, yet in Ezekiel 34 God promises Israel to bring them out of anarchy through a Davidic figure (Ezek 34:23), while in Ezekiel 37 the Davidic figure rules over Israel (Ezek 37:24). Simply put, the Davidic figure is the coming ruler who will embody the rule of Yahweh.[52] He will combine the theocratic and Messianic reigns and will lead Israel into the full restoration of the covenant relationship. The pertinent relationship has to be through the Messiah and in a theocratic format, not a democratic one. It is the rule of one God through one king over one covenantal people. They are not Judah and Ephraim, for they are now called Israel. Further, the restoration is possible not only through the Davidic figure, but also through the work of the Spirit of God in which we encounter the language of resurrection from the graves and recreation.

50. Allen, *Ezekiel 20–48*; Ezek 33:23–24.
51. Wright, *Message of Ezekiel*, 273–314. See esp. 310.
52. Ibid., 280.

In summary, we agree with Seitz who says that the "biological reality is inherently a theological reality."[53] Ezekiel is not saying that Israel will be restored to their land regardless of their covenantal faithfulness. Instead, he is stating that none can be restored to the covenantal blessings except through the work of the Davidic figure and the re-creation of the Spirit of God.

In other words, Ezekiel 33–37, as well as other texts, pictures a situation in which there is an obedient occupying party and a wicked dispossessed party. If the new inhabitants disobey God then they will be scattered among the nations. Only those who repent will come back, for no one can legitimately be in the land unless he or she is in harmony with God. By disobeying God, the northern kingdom lost her land in 722 BC. There is no inheritance without meeting the biblical requirements of justice and righteousness. In view of this teaching, any credible argument for the prophetic place of modern Israel should provide a theological justification for the moral state of Israel and for the displacement of hundreds of thousands of Palestinian refugees who lost their homes in 1948.[54] These refugees are the people whom God created and loved. Fifty thousand of them were Christians. The number of the Palestinian Christian refugees alone is huge in view of the number of exiles mentioned in Jeremiah, i.e., 3,023 exiles in 597 BC, 832 in 587 BC, and 745 in 582 BC (Jer 52:28–30).[55] Altogether 4,600 people were deported. Why would God take the Palestinian church into exile in order to bring a group of people who don't accept Jesus Christ as their Savior and Lord?

Our discussion of the claim that God gave Israel her land shows that this claim does not pay sufficient attention to the territorial fluidity of the land; to the notion that biblical Israel is a non-exclusive ethnic group; or to the moral requirements for dwelling in the land. Rather, there is a better biblical alternative that allows for the territorial and ethnic fluidities without overlooking the standards of holiness required to inhabit the land. The alternative is this: Christ is the owner of the land. Let us continue our study by looking at the meanings of the word "land."

53. Seitz, "Ezekiel 37:1–14," 53.

54. For further information, see Burge, *Whose Land? Whose Promise?*.

55. Even if we take the figures mentioned in 2 Kgs 24:14, 16 (10,000 people) as the number of exiles in 597 BC, the number of Christian Palestinian refugees is still five times more than this number.

three

The Land

An Alternative Perception

THE HISTORY OF RESEARCH on the theology of the land demonstrates that biblical scholars have moved away from limiting the concept of land to just one meaning.[1] Furthermore, land can be studied from more than one ideological perspective.[2] In simple words, scholars rightly assert that the meaning of the land depends on its historical, cultural, and theological contexts and requires a plurality of approaches in order to unpack it.[3] In

---

1. In 1966, in *The Problem of the Hexateuch and Other Essays*, von Rad distinguished between the historical and the cultic concepts. Consequently, he paved the way for studying the plural meanings of the land in Scriptures. Later, in the 1970s, Davies wrote a comprehensive monograph titled *The Gospel and the Land* in which he surveyed the data of the Old Testament, Apocrypha, Pseudepigrapha, Rabbinic sources, and the New Testament. He concluded that there are two main strata. In one stratum, the land, Jerusalem, and the temple are negative and even rejected on occasion. In this stratum, there is freedom from space. The opposite is true in the other stratum.

2. Brueggemann picked up the concern with space and the multiple aspects of the land. Using the social scientific method, he advances the theology of the land especially in his book *The Land*. He develops a biblical theology highlighting landedness and landlessness as dialectical aspects, and argues that the land cannot be reduced to mere physical dirt or to a spiritual metaphor. In the mid-1990s, Habel developed Bruggemann's work in his book *The Land Is Mine*, arguing that the Bible has six ideologies of the land (Royal, Theocratic, Ancestral-Household, Prophetic, Agrarian, and Immigrant). He clearly moves from a monolithic concept of the land to a spectrum of land ideologies.

3. Scholars continue to develop the perception of the multiple aspects of the land advocated by Brueggemann. More recent works include Burge, *Jesus and the Land*; Tarazi, *Land and Covenant*; Munayer, "Theology of the Land," 234–64. Burge is an American Evangelical New Testament scholar, Tarazi is a Palestinian Orthodox scholar, and Munayer is a Palestinian Evangelical Christian.

the following, we will focus on the ownership of the land and some of the meanings relevant to it.

The ownership of a specific land cannot be understood without a theology that perceives God as the ultimate Creator and Owner of the whole earth (Genesis 1). He is the one who entrusted it to humanity. Indeed, in defining the land in Scripture, we must consider the human and the divine, the anthropological and the theological. Anthropologically, the bond between the land and the human race is emphasized because of culture and agriculture. Theologically, the land has functional roles, such as reflecting God's blessing or curse. Like the human race, the land lives out salvation history. It suffered when sin entered and it will experience renewal through redemption. When its possessors ignored God and lived in sin, it experienced the curses of God, but when they followed God, it experienced rest, signifying an ontological change. In other words, the meaning and nature of the land are strongly associated with the nature of its masters. Whenever injustice dominates, the land suffers and its inhabitants are not at peace; but whenever its inhabitants are godly, it flourishes and overflows with blessings.

Therefore, its legitimate owners/inheritors determine its nature, for the land was made for man, not the other way around. If the owners are thieves, then it is a land of thieves. On the other hand, it could be a land of righteousness, and whenever its inheritors are righteous, it signifies a place of rest. Indeed, many references in the Wisdom literature of Scripture associate the land with the absence of evildoers and the inheritance of the righteous ones. Proverbs 2:21–22 says, "For the upright will live in the land, and the blameless will remain in it; but the wicked will be cut off from the land, and the unfaithful will be torn from it." Proverbs 10:30 says, "The righteous will never be uprooted, but the wicked will not remain in the land." Further, when Isaiah describes the land in a state of rest, he uses images of new creation where peace and security prevail (Isaiah 11). A survey of the inheritors/owners of the land in Scripture should open up new windows for understanding it.[4] At the risk of oversimplification, we

---

4. The Bible presents a long list of the owners of the land. The list includes God (Gen 1:1; Lev 25:23; Josh 22:19; Ps 24:1), Adam and Eve (Gen 1:26, 28–30), the family of Noah (Gen 9:1–7), one or more of the children of Noah (Gen 10:25), the Canaanites (Gen 10:19; 12:5; 23:2; Deut 1:7; 11:30; 32:49), a list of nations that ranges from three to ten members (Gen 15:19; Exod 3:17; Exod 23:28; Neh 9:8), Abraham and his descendants along with many nations (Gen 13:15; 15:7, 18; 17:8; 22:17), Isaac and descendants along with many nations (Gen 26:3), Jacob and descendants along with many nations (Gen

will study the relevant data in three stages: the land before Abraham, the land and Abraham, and the land and Christ.

The Land before Abraham

In this era, the focus is not on the land of Canaan but on the whole earth. The Hebrew term for land can refer to: planet earth; the earth without the waters; or the people of the world. The following examples should illustrate this point.

> In the beginning God created the heavens and the earth. (Gen 1:1)

> God saw how corrupt the earth had become, for all the people on earth had corrupted their ways. (Gen 6:12)

> Now the whole world [land] had one language and a common speech. (Gen 11:1)

Further, in a brief study of the usages and contexts of the land in Genesis 1–11, we see first in Genesis 1 that God is its Creator and Owner. Then, God entrusts it to the human race. Genesis 1:28–30 says,

> God blessed them and said to them, "Be fruitful and increase in number; fill the earth and subdue it. Rule over the fish of the sea and the birds of the air and over every living creature that moves on the ground." Then God said, "I give you every seed-bearing plant on the face of the whole earth and every tree that has fruit with seed in it. They will be yours for food. And to all the beasts of the earth and all the birds of the air and all the creatures that move on the ground—everything that has the breath of life in it—I give every green plant for food." And it was so.

At that time there were only two people, Adam and Eve. God put them in Eden, the incubator of the human race—the center of the world—and entrusted the whole earth to them (Gen 1:27–30; 2:8). He placed them in

---

28:4, 13; 35:12; 48:4), the Israelites along with many other nations (cf. the books of Joshua + Judges), the united kingdom, and other nations (cf. 1 & 2 Sam and 1 Kgs), the divided kingdom and other nations (cf. 1 & 2 Kgs), the Assyrian Empire and Judah (2 Kgs 17; Isa 7–8, 36–37), the Babylonian Empire (cf. Jer; 2 Kgs 25), the Persian Empire (cf. Ezra/Neh), the Greek Empire and the Hasmonians (cf. the Intertestamental literature, the Apocrypha), the Roman Empire (cf. the New Testament), Jesus Christ (Matt 28:18–20; John 1:3; Phil 2:10; Col 1:15–20; Heb 1:1–4), Abraham (Rom 4:13), the meek (Matt 5:5), and the children of God (Gal 3:29; Rev 21:1–9).

Eden and asked them to work there (Gen 2:15) because it was the best place to fulfill his plan for the whole earth and to live in harmony with him. Unfortunately, because the humans disobeyed God and ate the fruit of the forbidden tree, the Lord expelled them from Eden. The non-inclusive language of the NIV points out this expulsion saying,

> So the Lord God banished him from the Garden of Eden to work the ground from which he had been taken. After he drove the man out, he placed on the east side of the Garden of Eden cherubim and a flaming sword flashing back and forth to guard the way to the tree of life. (Gen 3:23–24)

From Genesis 1–11 we see that moving eastward is associated with trouble (cf. Gen 3:24, 4:16, 10:25, 30, 11:2). For example, the Bible tells us that when Cain killed his brother Abel, he "went out from the Lord's presence and lived in the Land of Nod, **east** of Eden" (Gen 3:24).[5] Accessibility to Eden was closed, not only because of the cherubim and the flaming sword (Gen 3:24), but also because of sin. Sin alienated the human race from God, and consequently, mankind lived without peace with God and experienced the curse of the whole earth.

After the human race multiplied, it provoked God to anger culminating in the destruction of the whole earth by the flood. Noah and his family survived and repopulated the earth, but children were born in a sinful state, alienated from God. This demographic change influenced the identity of the land and shifted the emphasis from the whole earth to specific places. The singular word for "earth" becomes plural. The plural form of the word "land/earth" appears for the first time in Genesis 10 and speaks of the lands of Japheth (Gen 10:5), Ham (Gen 10:20), and Shem (Gen 10:31). In addition, there are several divisions within each one of them. The descendants of Ham deserve special attention, for their lands became the focus of many subsequent texts.

First, Canaan, son of Ham, occupies lands that are important to the children of Israel. Canaan's land is the only place where we find explicit borders in primeval history apart from Eden. The book of Genesis tells us: "the borders of Canaan reached from Sidon toward Gerar as far as Gaza, and then toward Sodom, Gomorrah, Admah and Zeboiim, as far as Lasha" (Gen 10:19). Sodom and Gomorrah are mentioned later in Genesis 14 and also in Genesis 19. They are clearly wicked cities under divine judgment.

5. I highlighted the word "east."

Second, Nimrod, a descendant of Ham, established the first human kingdom in Eretz Shinar (Gen 10:10). There, the whole earth participated in building the tower of Babel (Gen 11:1–9), provoking God's anger and his response. As they tried to ascend to reach God, God descended, confused their tongues, and scattered them. This is the biblical explanation for the existence of many languages, nations, and lands (cf. Gen 10:5, 20, 31). In other words, the plurality of languages and lands is understood in a theological framework as the result of sin. The real problem is not the plurality of lands, but sin. The former is only a result of the latter. It is the symptom, not the disease. As a result, any effective solutions must address the root of the problem—the curse of Adam when he disobeyed God. For because of him the land was cursed, and as his descendants followed in his footsteps, it experienced further divine judgment. The land can prosper only when righteousness prevails. Its redemption and the restoration of its unity are only possible when the remedy for its curse is found.

The Bible also presents Shem and his descendants in relation to the land. Following reference to Japeth and his lands (Gen 10:5), and Ham and his lands (Gen 10:20), the Bible mentions Shem and his lands (Gen 10:31). It is interesting to note Peleg, one of Shem's descendants. In his time the land was divided.[6] The text says, "Two sons were born to Eber: One was named Peleg, because in his time the earth was divided" (Gen 10:25). The Hebrew verb "divide" occurs four times in the Old Testament (Gen 10:25; 1 Chron 1:19; Ps 55:9; Job 38:25).[7] The texts in both Genesis and Chronicles are identical. It is also interesting that Psalm 55:10 uses this Hebrew verb to denote confusion of tongues. It says, "Confuse the wicked, O Lord, confound their speech, for I see violence and strife in the city." The Hebrew text literally says: "divide their tongues." Thus, Genesis 10:25 in light of its context (cf. Gen 11:1) could imply that the division of the land is related to the division of tongues. This conclusion is also supported by the connection of the division of lands and tongues in Genesis 10:5, 20, and 31. Further, the connection between chapters 10 and 11 has not only been established by the genealogy of Shem (Gen 10:21–31; 11:10–32); the move to the land of Canaan (Gen 10:19; 11:31); and the *waw* consecutive (operates as conjunction in the Hebrew text) at the beginning of chapter 11; but also by the geographical location for both the kingdom of Nimrod and the building of the tower of Babel in the land of Shinar (Gen 10:10; 11:2).

6. Peleg and the Hebrew word for divided (*niflega*) come from the same root: *plg*.

7. Please note that the Hebrew reference for Ps 55:9 is Ps 55:10.

In short, neither the cursed Canaan (Gen 9:25), nor his nephew, the mighty Nimrod (Gen 10:9), nor the builders of the tower of Babel (Genesis 11) can reunite the divided earth. Such a task can be accomplished neither by might nor by human power. It can be accomplished only by the intervention of God through a descendant of Shem. Through the seed of Abram, we are told, God will redeem the land and restore its unity and blessing.

The Land and Abraham

Genesis 12:1–3 is a pivotal text. Structurally, the text is divided into two sets. The Hebrew text is as follows:

לֶךְ־לְךָ מֵאַרְצְךָ וּמִמּוֹלַדְתְּךָ וּמִבֵּית אָבִיךָ

וְאֶעֶשְׂךָ לְגוֹי גָּדוֹל וַאֲבָרֶכְךָ וַאֲגַדְּלָה שְׁמֶךָ

וֶהְיֵה בְּרָכָה

וַאֲבָרֲכָה מְבָרֲכֶיךָ וּמְקַלֶּלְךָ אָאֹר וְנִבְרְכוּ בְךָ כֹּל מִשְׁפְּחֹת הָאֲדָמָה:

The English equivalent is:

I. Leave your land, your kindred, and the house of your father to the land that I will show you then I shall make you into a great nation, bless you, and make your name great.

II. Be a blessing so that I can bless those who bless you; curse those who curse you, and that all the families of the earth can be blessed in you.[8]

Both sets in Hebrew have similar syntax, alliterations, and rhymes. The rhyme is shown with a double underline and it is related to the second masculine pronoun that sounds like "ka." It occurs ten times. The alliteration has a solid underline. It occurs three times in every set. Both sets have a similar syntax. The set starts with an imperative followed by an imperfective. It is surprising that many English translations miss the imperative at the beginning of the second set. God commands Abram: "be a blessing." The NIV text chooses to translate the imperative form as a future result: "you will be a blessing." However, the American Standard Version translates the Hebrew text as "be thou a blessing." The imperative force is so obvious in Hebrew that it is unacceptable to ignore it, especially in light of the division of the text into two sets by means of the imperative verb.

8. The translation is my own.

In short, the text highlights the idea of blessing through the repetition of the word "bless" five times, and through the grammatical shift in Hebrew syntax in which the imperfect changes into a perfect form – "all the families of the earth can be blessed in you."

The text does not claim an unconditional grant of land to Abram, let alone to his descendants. The imperative force at the beginning of the second set followed by a *waw* consecutive and an imperfect requires a conditional interpretation of verses 2–3. Further, the focus is not on the land but on divine blessing that through Abram overflows to the ends of the earth. Abram is going to be a blessing. However, even though he built altars unto the Lord (Gen 12:7–8) there was a severe famine in the land (Gen 12:10), reminding us of its curse (Gen 3:17–19) and of the need for God's redemption. This divine redemption will be accomplished through Abram's seed.

In other words, in Genesis 12 God shows Abram the land under his custody. In Genesis 13 Abram sees the land that he and his seed are supposed to inherit. In Genesis 15 God gives further details about it. And in Genesis 22:17 God declares that the dominion of the seed of Abraham will extend to include all the territories of their enemies. The text says: "I will surely bless you and make your descendants as numerous as the stars in the sky and as the sand on the seashore. Your descendants will take possession of the cities of their enemies" (Gen 22:17). It seems that the land of Abraham is not going to have fixed borders. It will continue to expand as it conquers the gates of the enemies, thus increasing in size both territorially and demographically. The land of Abraham will continue to extend until it is equal to the whole earth. Its inhabitants will be as numerous as the sand of the seashore and the stars of heaven for God's intention was not to set fixed borders, but to unite the ends of the earth under the Abrahamic banner. Thus, the many lands will become one through Abraham's seed. This divine vision is present, not only during the Abrahamic era, but also during and after the Davidic period. A quick look at the book of Psalms suffices to illustrate this point. In Psalm 2, God says to his Anointed One, "I will make the nations your inheritance, the ends of the earth your possession" (Ps 2:8). Clearly, God did not intend to isolate Abraham or his descendants from the rest of the world. On the contrary, God wanted a theocratic kingdom filled with Abraham's children.

Israel, however, preferred to have a human king like the rest of the nations (1 Samuel 8). This shift initiated a new era in which the Davidic dynasty appears. Nevertheless, it did not abolish the global aspect of God's promises. Gladly, many voices contextualized the hope that the Abrahamic land would still encompass the whole earth. Zion and its temple would become the center of their world. Isaiah writes that all the nations will come to Zion to the house of the Lord (Isa 2:1–4). Psalm 87 proclaims that different nations will become citizens of Zion.[9] The nations are born again in Zion and they are now part of a community that values the city of God and lives in it.[10] They have become part of a multiethnic and multicultural group whose legitimate differences are not stronger than their loyalty to the God of Zion.[11] Zion hosts all of them and her God grants them local citizenship without any biases. All are considered equal by birth. They could obtain permanent inheritance and enjoy the continuous support of the community of God.[12] According to Sparks, this vision fits an ancient Near Eastern mentality of empires or global kingdoms which are, by nature, multiethnic and not tribal or parochial. Sparks' comments on this issue are relevant to our discussion. He writes,

> For the Egyptians and Assyrians, identity was political and cultural, not ethnic, and was linked with kingship, the king's relationship to the deity, and the deity's role in extending the national borders and the native empire to the "ends of the earth."[13]

9. Since the times of David, Zion acquired special importance. Geographically, it referred to the Temple Mount (Ps 20:2; Joel 4:17, 21), the whole of Jerusalem (Isa 2:3, 33:14; Joel 2:32), or to Judea (Isa 10:24, 51:11). Figuratively, it is associated with the people of Judah, or the people of God (Isa 51:16; 59:20). Furthermore, the New Testament associated it with the heavenly Jerusalem (Gal 4:21–31) and thus facilitated restoring the importance of Zion theology, utilizing eschatological imageries and reminding us of the cosmic dimension of Zion declared in the Old Testament.

10. The transformation of the nations is an important ingredient of Zion theology. John Strong explains that Zion theology includes five motifs: (1) Mount Zion is associated with Mount Zaphon, (2) a river flows out of Zion, (3) Yahweh conquers chaos, (4) Yahweh provides security to Jerusalem, and (5) the nations are transformed; they come to Zion to acknowledge Yahweh's sovereignty. Strong, "Zion," in VanGemeren, *New International Dictionary*, 4:1314.

11. Elsewhere I have provided a detailed study of Psalm 87 in which I show how the nations are transformed in the pertinent psalm. For further details, see Katanacho, "Jerusalem Is the City of God," 181–99.

12. Knauth provides a good summary of the status of aliens in ancient Israel. He informs us that generally aliens did not obtain permanent inheritance and lacked family ties. Knauth, "Alien, Foreign Resident," 32.

13. Sparks, *Ethnicity and Identity*, 91.

The identity of these empires is not controlled by ethnicity, but by a linkage to a deity.[14] Their main organizing principle is not consanguinity but a socio-religious identity. If this vision is also God's vision for the world, then it follows that Israel's identity and land is not fixed, but should be continually expanding. This conclusion is congruent with the study of Wazana who proposes that some descriptions of the borders of the promised land in the Bible are "literary descriptions."[15] These descriptions are a spatial merism that refers to the whole world. Merism is a literary device that denotes totality by contrasting the parts.

THE LAND AND CHRIST

Several authors have used the New Testament to address the issue of the land. W. D. Davies argues that it has been "Christified."[16] William Blanchard furthers Davies and von Rad's arguments, describing the nature of Christ's ministry as "christifying" space, and pointing out that the focus of Jesus was Jerusalem and worship. Peter Walker picks up this issue, and based on Paul, Hebrews, John, Luke-Acts, and Revelation, concludes that the land is subsumed in the New Testament under God's purposes for the whole world. In doing so, he connects the theme of the land to salvation history.[17]

The latter is indeed a helpful framework in both Old and New Testaments. Within this framework, the New Testament has important contributions to make concerning the ownership and borders of the land.[18] The New Testament teaches that Jesus is the second Adam. It says: "The first man Adam became a living being; the last Adam, a life-giving spirit (1 Cor 15:45). As with Adam, God entrusted Christ with the whole earth. The Bible says:

> God blessed them and said to them, "Be fruitful and increase in number; fill the earth and subdue it. Rule over the fish of the sea

14. We can see a similar notion of identity in the early spread of Islam.

15. Wazana, "From Dan to Beer-Sheba," 45–85. See also the Hebrew book of Wazana, *All the Boundaries of the Land*.

16. Davies has influenced my thinking, especially in his books *The Gospel and the Land* and *The Territorial Dimension of Judaism*.

17. Walker, "Land in the Apostles' Writings," 98.

18. The New Testament authors universalized the concept of the land. Instead of the land of Israel they use the whole earth.

> and the birds of the air and over every living creature that moves on the ground." (Gen 1:28)

> Then Jesus came to them and said, "All authority in heaven and on earth has been given to me." (Matt 28:18)

This turning point in redemptive history, according to D. A. Carson, signifies that the sphere of Christ's authority includes all earth.[19] Carson labels it as "absolute authority"; Donald Hagner calls it "comprehensive sovereignty"; and Robert Gundry describes it as "universal authority."[20] Simply stated, Christ has ownership rights over the whole earth, including the Middle East. This ownership was declared in the first century after Christ's birth after all the promises of the Old Testament had been given. In accordance with progressive revelation, Christ is now the owner of the whole earth, even though God had entrusted it to Abraham and his descendants in the past. Christ owns it because he is the Abrahamic seed and the fulfillment of prophecy.

Paul supports this understanding, stating that Christ is the king of the whole earth, for every knee will bow down to him (Phil 2:10). All things were created by him and for him (Col 1:16). He is the ultimate goal and the divine means. Curtis Vaughan writes that Christ shaped the physical and theological identities of the earth, and the latter reflects some of his characteristics.[21] He is the means by which earth was created. Theologically, the land must be understood in a christological framework. It is no longer defined by the Abrahamic promises, for Christ is the one whom God made as the heir of everything. The Bible says: "In the past God spoke to our forefathers through the prophets at many times and in various ways, but in these last days he has spoken to us by his Son, whom he appointed heir of all things, and through whom he made the universe (Heb 1:1–2). Morris asserts that "heir" means one who gains lawful possession.[22] The author of Hebrews is thus claiming that Christ is the lawful heir of everything. He adopts an Old Testament teaching advocating God's anointed one as the rightful heir and challenging all those who consider the emperor to be the heir of all things.[23] The simple claim is that Christ would receive the nations

19. Carson, "Matthew," 594.

20. Ibid., 594; Hagner, *Matthew 14–28*, 886; Gundry, *Matthew*, 595.

21. Vaughan, "Colossians," 182.

22. Morris, "Hebrews," 13.

23. Koester, *Hebrews*, 185.

as his inheritance and the ends of the earth as his possession (Ps 2:7–8; Ps 89:26). More specifically, it is an everlasting possession, as the Greek word for heir, according to Elingworth, indicates permanent possession, usually of land.[24]

The New Testament demonstrates that Christ is the Abrahamic seed in which and through which the promises are fulfilled. Through him, the Abrahamic land extends to the whole earth. In fact, Abraham himself, believed in Jesus (John 8:56) and through faith he became the heir of the whole world. The promise to Abraham was not to have a land with fixed borders, but to inherit the whole earth. Paul says: "It was not through law that Abraham and his offspring received the promise that he would be heir of the world, but through the righteousness that comes by faith" (Rom 4:13). Commenting on Romans 4:13, Bailey says that even though Paul knew the Septuagint well, he felt free to replace the word "*ge*," the Greek equivalent of land/earth, with "cosmos" or the whole world, in order to highlight the cosmic dimension of the Abrahamic promises; Paul is clearly expanding the promises of land mentioned in Genesis 12:7 and 17:8.[25] Bailey adds that in the intertestamental period the territorial promise is either universalized or spiritualized. He supports his argument by several examples, such as Jubilees 32:16–26, Ben Sirach 44:21.[26]

> And I shall give to thy seed all the earth which is under heaven, and they will judge all the nations according to their desires, and after that they will get possession of the whole earth and inherit it forever. (Jubilees 32:19)

> God promised him with an oath that in his descendants the nations would be blessed, That he would make him numerous as the grains of dust, and exalt his posterity like the stars; That he would give them an inheritance from sea to sea, and from the River to the ends of the earth. (Ben Sirach 44:21 NAB)

Bailey is right in seeing the universal dimension of the land. However, it seems to us that this universality or this global vision for the children of Abraham has existed since the birth of the Abrahamic promises (Gen 12:3;

24. Ellingworth, *Epistle to the Hebrews*, 94–95.

25. Bailey, "St. Paul's Understanding of the Territorial Promise," 60.

26. The Book of Jubilees is a text from the second century BC that covers much of the same ground as Genesis, with some interesting additional details. For further details, see "Book of Jubilees," n.p.

22:17). The biblical data demonstrates that the concept of the borders of the land has been fluid since its inception, and that God wanted to reach to the ends of the earth. This vision is only possible through Christ, for he alone is the ultimate owner of the land, a place that is not made up of mere dirt but is a locale where righteousness and justice should prevail. No wonder Christ proclaimed that "the meek shall inherit the land" (Matt 5:5; cf. Ps 37:11). The meek, not the strong, aggressive, harsh, or tyrannical will enter the land and inherit it.[27] This approach is congruent to many assertions within the Old Testament. The following examples should illustrate this point:

> Hear now, O Israel, the decrees and laws I am about to teach you. Follow them so that you may live and may go in and take possession of the land that the Lord, the God of your fathers, is giving you. (Deut 4:1)

> Follow justice and justice alone, so that you may live and possess the land the LORD your God is giving you. (Deut 16:20)

> When you cry out for help, let your collection of idols save you! The wind will carry all of them off, a mere breath will blow them away. But the man who makes me his refuge will inherit the land and possess my holy mountain. (Isa 57:13)

These texts affirm that inheriting the land is associated with righteousness, justice, and obedience. A right relationship with God is indispensable for possessing and enjoying the land. "Meek" refers to the humble person who depends upon the Lord. Further, according to Carson, "there is no need to interpret the land metaphorically, as having no reference to geography or space."[28] In other words, the land is not only literal but its legitimate inhabitants are characterized by godly qualities. In Paul's words, "If you belong to Christ, then you are Abraham's seed, and heirs according to the promise" (Gal 3:29). Paul, here, is refuting the Judaizers' claim that becoming part of the physical seed of Abraham through circumcision secures one's inclusion in the Abrahamic promises.[29] Christ alone is the legitimate seed of Abraham in whom the promises will be fulfilled (Gal 3:16). To be associated with him is the only legitimate means to belong to the seed of Abraham and consequently, to the Abrahamic promises. Therefore, any

27. Carson, "Matthew," 133.
28. Ibid.
29. Boice, "Galatians," 469.

theological claims that replace Christ's ownership with Israel's must deal with the difficulties of defining Israel, and with the New Testament claims that Christ has received the Abrahamic inheritance of the land.

CONCLUDING REMARKS

We have provided a biblical framework for questioning any theological system that promotes a higher status for one nation over another, hoping to encourage the reader to study the concerns presented in the previous pages.

Accepting that Christ is the owner of the land and we, the inhabitants of the land, are its stewards, it follows that we must honor God in his land by affirming the unique mission of the elected land. It is a land of faith, peace, reconciliation, and hope. Any solution to the Arab–Israeli conflict must take the mission of the land into consideration. Any political solution must reflect justice, righteousness, and biblical love for both Palestinians and Israelis. It must empathize with the oppressed whether they are Palestinians or Israelis, Arabs or Jews. This understanding prompted me to participate in writing the Palestinian Kairos Document, which guides Christians as stewards of the land that Christ owns, and in addressing the Israeli occupation in a biblical way. The next section will address the theological contribution of the Kairos Document.

four

The Kairos Theology

In this section, I will talk about the Palestinian Kairos Document.[1] It is important to introduce the document by clarifying two important terms in its title: "Palestinian" and "Kairos Document."

Most regrettably, stereotyping abounds and there are numerous misunderstandings related to certain words. Thus, although many are aware of the differences between the labels Muslim, Arab, and Palestinian, it is still important to point out some of the pertinent differences. The word "Palestinian" is frequently misunderstood.[2] This word is not Arabic in origin, but rather, is etymologically associated with the Philistines who are ethnically and culturally distinct from modern Palestinians.[3] It refers to a group of

1. The Palestinian Kairos Document is available online: www.kairospalestine.ps. It is also available in the addendum. I will refer to the document as the Kairos Document. Also, although I am one of the authors of the Kairos Document, I present my own reading of the document in this section. I extrapolate and expand certain points that are implicit in the Kairos Document, drawing from the long conversations that the Kairos authors had during our meetings. It goes without saying that I am alone responsible for the content of this section.

2. It is unfortunate that the Van Dyck-Smith Arabic Bible translates the label "Philistines" as Palestinians. This Bible is the most dominant one in the Arab world. Sadly, every time I explain the story of David and Goliath to an Arab Palestinian audience, I have to explain that God is not against Palestinians and that the label "Palestinian" is not tantamount to the label Philistines. For further details, see Smith and Van Dyck, *Arabic Van Dyck Bible*. Gladly, we note that more recent Arabic translations are taking these differences into consideration.

3. Further details about the ethnicities of the Palestinian community are found in Sabella, "Religious and Ethnic Communities," 346–49.

people who are culturally Arab and geographically or historically related to the land between the Jordan River and the Mediterranean Sea. A Palestinian might be Christian or Muslim or Druze, and in a period of history there were Jewish Palestinians. Moreover, I present the following assertions to clarify major components in the identity of Palestinian Arab Christians. First, not all Arabs are Muslims. Arabs existed before Islam.[4] Clearly, the term Arab or one of its cognates is mentioned sixteen times in the Old Testament, eight times in the Maccabean books, and three times in the New Testament.[5] The pertinent term appears in Scripture as far back as Solomon (1 Kgs 10:15). In extra-biblical works, it appears as early as 867 BC.[6]

Second, not all Muslims are Arabs. Some Muslims, for example, are Indonesian. Third, not all Arabs are Palestinians. The Arab world is full of other Arabs, such as Jordanians, Iraqis, Syrians, or others. Fourth, not all Palestinians live under Israeli occupation. In addition to the Palestinians living in the West Bank and Gaza Strip, there are other Palestinians. Some Palestinians live in Europe, America, and several Arab countries. Furthermore, some Palestinians are Israelis. In fact, more than 20 percent of Israel's citizens are Palestinian Israelis, who are mainly striving for equality and a state that represents all of its citizens, Palestinian and Jewish Israelis alike. Fifth, not all Palestinian Christians are in theological agreement. There are four church families amongst Palestinian Christians (Orthodox, Oriental Orthodox, Catholic, and Protestants). The Kairos Document does not

4. My affirmation of a pre-Islamic Arab identity is not rooted in an Islamophobic attitude. Instead, it provides a wider perspective for understanding the history of Arab Muslims as well as Christians. Shahid has provided a well-documented study about Arab Christians before Islam. Shahid, *Byzantium and the Arabs in the Fifth Century*; *Rome and the Arabs*; *Byzantium and the Arabs in the Sixth Century*; and *Byzantium and the Arabs in the Fourth Century*. See also Trimingham, *Christianity among the Arabs in Pre-Islamic Times*; Cragg, *The Arab Christian*.

5. Apart from direct quotations, I will use the labels Old Testament and New Testament to refer to the two parts of the Protestant Bible. In addition, further information about the label Arab is found in Katanacho, "Label Arab in the Old Testament," 1–11. Also see the following references: 1 Kgs 10:15; 2 Chron 9:14; 17:11; 21:16; 22:1; 26:7; Neh 2:19; 4:7; 6:1; Isa 13:20; 21:13 (twice); Jer 3:2; 25:24 (twice); Ezra 27:21. The label "Arab" appears in deuterocanonical books such as: 1 Mac 5:39; 11:15, 17, 39; 12:31; 2 Mac 5:8; 12:10, 11) as well as in the New Testament (Acts 2:11; Gal 1:17; 4:25). In fact, John the Baptist lost his life defending an Arab woman. He rebuked Herod Antipas who was not satisfied with his own wife. His wife was the daughter of Aretas IV who ruled the Nabatean Arabs from 9 BC–AD 40. She was an Arab.

6. Pritchard, *Ancient Near Eastern Texts Relating to the Old Testament*, 278–79. See also Israel Eph'al, *Ancient Arabs*, 1–3. See also Retsö, *Arabs in Antiquity*, 105.

necessarily represent all Palestinian theologians, let alone all Christians living in Israel/Palestine, yet it has a wide acceptance and is supported by all the patriarchs and heads of churches in Jerusalem.[7]

Next, it is fitting to clarify the meaning of the word "Kairos." The Palestinian Kairos Document was inspired, in part, by the South African Kairos Document launched in 1985.[8] The Palestinian Kairos Document was written by theologians and human rights activists from different denominations and launched in December 2009. In the Palestinian Kairos Document, Christian Palestinians present a list of various oppressive Israeli measures taken against Palestinians as they seek the triune God and aim to fight injustice and advocate the kingdom of God in Israel/Palestine.

This does not mean that Palestinians have never sinned against Israelis or that Palestinian Christians are apathetic towards Jewish pain. In fact, several Palestinians, including myself, have condemned suicide bombing as well as other forms of violence that spill innocent Israeli Jewish blood. At the same time, it is important to understand that the pertinent document is a Palestinian cry that comes out of pain, hurt, and an unbearable occupation. Occupation is the main problem and violence is its fruit, not vice versa. Anyway, the Palestinian Kairos Document presents the Palestinian Christian narrative that has been overlooked by many Christians.

This widely supported document is an interdenominational, theological document that describes the Palestinian–Israeli conflict in biblical categories and in a context of suffering. It is called the Kairos Document because many Palestinian Christians believe that the decisive and appointed divine time, "the *Kairos*," has come for the Palestinian church to speak out as one body.[9] The document reflects on some of the major Palestinian con-

---

7. Most Messianic Jews, for example, have neither endorsed nor welcomed the Kairos Document. Admittedly, the Kairos Document does not address their concerns. Also, the Kairos Document does not discuss what has happened in Christian-Jewish relations. We hope that further discussions will develop with Jews as well as Messianic Jews in the future. Further, the label "Israel/Palestine" refers to the land that was occupied by Israel in 1948 and then in 1967. In this section, the label "occupation" refers to Israel's control of the land that was taken in 1967 and not to the land that was taken in 1948.

8. The South African Kairos Document can be found online: www.sahistory.org.za/pages/library-resources/officialdocs/kairos-document.htm. For further information, see Biyela, "Beyond the Kairos Document"; Petersen, "Time, Resistance and Reconstruction"; Van der Water, "The Legacy of a Prophetic Moment"; Villa-Vicencio, *Theology & Violence.*

9. For a study of the meaning of the word "Kairos," see Kittel et al., *Theological Dictionary of the New Testament,* 389.

cerns providing a good window for understanding Palestinian Christians and for observing some of their recent theological as well as methodological developments.[10] It is a document that reflects the identity of the Palestinian church in Israel/Palestine and shares its message. It points out its hermeneutical reflections affirming not only theological beliefs, but also hermeneutical concerns. The latter is our starting point, and subsequently, we will encounter the document's perception of Trinitarian theology, theology of the land, theology of resistance and eschatology.

HERMENEUTICS IN THE KAIROS DOCUMENT

Miroslav Volf asserts that "method is message."[11] Indeed, theological method and discipline cannot be separated from one another. From this point of view, it is important to observe that the Kairos Document starts with context and then addresses doctrinal beliefs before interpretation of the Scriptures. All of these components are theology. This principle is essential for understanding the interaction of faith and politics or the theopolitical endeavors in the Kairos Document. There is no doubt that the theological contribution of the Kairos Document is beyond foundationalism.[12] The expression "beyond foundationalism" is used by Stanley Grenz and John Franke in their attempt to expound theology in a postmodern world.[13] In a postmodern context, some Palestinian theologians have moved away from liberalism, in which the world absorbs the text and subdues it, to post-liberalism in which the biblical text redescribes the world in biblical categories. The Kairos Document does not dwell on describing empire. It does not try to deconstruct political colonial programs by proof–texting. Instead of restructuring the biblical reality in order to make it congruent to our experience, the Kairos Document describes the Palestinian–Israeli conflict in biblical categories (love, justice, hope, etc.). From this perspec-

10. For a survey of different Palestinian theological approaches, see Katanacho, "Palestinian Protestant Theological Responses," 289–305. In this article, you will find four different Palestinian approaches: the biographies, the apologies, liberation theology, and reconciliation theologies (Sulah and Musalaha).

11. Volf, "Theology, Meaning & Power," 45.

12. At the risk of oversimplification, foundationalism is a theory of knowledge that affirms that derivative beliefs are founded on more basic beliefs, i.e., foundational beliefs. Basic beliefs are not justified by other beliefs.

13. Grenz and Franke, *Beyond Foundationalism.*

tive, the document focuses on faith, love, hope, the mission of the church, and the mission of the land. It mirrors a worldview that reflects critically and constructively on our identity, reality, faith, and practices, and seeks to articulate a theological discourse that assists the community of followers of Christ to live out their calling in Israel/Palestine in the twenty-first century. It also points us away from epistemology to ontology, reflecting on our identity as the people of God who are living in the midst of hatred, violence, conflict and suffering. Our identity is rooted in the identity of God for we are created in God's own image.

Our perception of God cannot be divorced from our commitment to the Bible, in both of its Testaments, as well as to the guidance of the Holy Spirit. The Kairos Document affirms that it "is the Spirit that helps us to understand Holy Scripture, both Old and New Testaments, showing their unity, here and now."[14] Our discussion in the Kairos group included the authority and the role of the Old Testament. We affirm that the Old Testament is the word of God and its contribution is indispensable. However, it must be understood in light of the contributions of the New Testament and the centrality of Jesus Christ. Jesus Christ is the ultimate fulfillment of the law and the prophets (Luke 24:44). He is our model for interpreting Scriptures properly. Like our Lord and the apostles, the Kairos Document does not reject any part of the Old Testament, thus affirming its unity with the New Testament. The two Testaments are one book and interpreting them together is the best approach for any Palestinian Christian. Indeed, the document reflects an implicit assertion that any rejection of the Old Testament is not admissible. The Old Testament is not only the book of the Jews but also the book of the church, including the Palestinian church. However, Christians should not understand it without Christ. The historical meaning of a particular text must be in dialogue with the canonical as well as the theological meanings of the whole Bible. Without this interaction, the meaning of a particular text has the potential of being distorted. The Christ Event has a central role in the canonical and theological meanings of the Bible, and biblical historiography is unashamedly theological. Theology and hermeneutics cannot be divorced, for the latter is not mere method. But what kind of theology should guide our hermeneutical enterprise? It seems that a Trinitarian theology is the best choice.

In addition, it is fitting to discuss the spectrum of approaches to the Bible and discuss the Kairos hermeneutical approach in relation to these

---

14. Kairos 2.1.2.

approaches. First, what do we mean by the "Bible"? Are we talking about the Old Testament or both testaments? What do we mean by the Old Testament? Does it include the deuterocanonical or apocryphal books and which ones? Obviously, the deuterocanonical books in different church families (Orthodox, Oriental Orthodox, and Catholic) are not identical![15] Furthermore, should we use the Hebrew text of the Old Testament or the Greek one, the Masoretic or the Septuagint text? Second, why are the approaches "to" the Bible? Are we assuming that the reader, or the community of readers, approach the Bible or does the Bible approach us? Is the direction of the process of interpretation from the reader to the text or the other way around or does it go both ways? Third, are we equating the Bible with the Word of God or is the former a vehicle of the latter?[16] Last, at least I can endorse without much resistance one component, i.e., the "s" in the word approaches. Indeed there are several approaches. I will point out few major approaches and point out few implications to the Palestinian-Israeli context. Then I will highlight the hermenutical approach of the Kairos Document in light of our understanding of other approaches.

First, there is the historical-critical approach. John Barton in "Historical-Critical Approaches" explains that many interpreters read the Bible with the following assumptions.[17] They ask genetic questions. When and by whom were the books written? What was their intended readership? They look for the original meaning. For example, what does the word "mirror" mean in the epistle of James or what does "justice" mean in the book of Psalms? They try to do historical reconstruction with a hermeneutics of suspicion. Moreover, they distinguish between what really happened and what the authors want us to believe. Last, they affirm that the best reading strategy is to have a disinterested reader who is neutral and objective.

Many of the genetic questions are related to identity. Who is the "true" Israel? Should we adopt a maximalist point of view of biblical history and believe in the historicity of Abraham, Moses, David, Joshua, and others? Should we accept that the biblical events are actual historical events? Others prefer a minimalist perception of biblical history and point out that

15. The term *deuterocanonical* has different connotations in different church traditions. The Armenian Orthodox Church, for example, has the book of Fourth Maccabean which is not accepted in the Greek Orthodox or Catholic traditions. The Greek Orthodox has Psalm 151 or First Esdras which is not found in the Catholic tradition. Furthermore, the Ethiopian church has books that are not accepted by all of the above. They have seven "extra" books in the New Testament.

16. See Meadowcroft, *Message of the Word of God*, 23–24.

17. Barton, "Historical-Critical Approaches," 9–20.

many biblical stories are simply ideological, political, literary, or mythological depictions? Many Israeli archeologists strive to establish a particular reading of biblical history in order to gain political advantage. Names of places are changed to ancient biblical names. On the other hand, such reading strategies put the Palestinian church at a disadvantage. They are perceived as the Canaanites or Philistines? Some Palestinians are tempted to delve into this history game and argue that they were in the land before the ancient children of Israel; as if an ancient historical presence is the basis for contemporary human rights including the right to own a home that might have inherited from your grandfather.

Second, there is the social scientific approach. In continuity with the historical critical method, several scholars wanted to reconstruct the pre-textual social world in order to understand and interpret the Bible properly. They emphasized the importance of sociology and anthropology. Their approaches have enriched our understanding of the text. However, most of them focused on Israel and its social world overlooking other inhabitants who lived in the land. The social world was constructed through the eyes of the privileged community and the marginalized nations in the land were overlooked or considered an inferior group whether ethically or religiously or in other aspects. Such depictions created a social conceptual grid that encouraged segregation and ethnocentricity. The current state of Israel continues to suffer from the latter. Admittedly, social scientific approaches are not the reason for Israel's ethnocentric perception but it facilitated accepting such beliefs.

Third, there is the literaty reading of the Bible. After failing to reconstruct the pre-textual reality, several scholars rightly moved into focusing on the text. New questions appeared; such as, what is the relationship between different texts, i.e., intertextuality? Several Israeli and Palestinian scholars highlighted the different literary dimensions of parts of the Bible. The literary approach freed the readers from the concerns of the absent author(s) or redactors. The synchronic study became prominent and attenuated the dominance of diachronic approaches. Consequently, the interest in the readers and their concerns escalated. This paved the way for poststructuralist and postmodern readings. One of the important consequences in the Israeli—Palestinian context is the political reading of the Bible.

Fourth, there is the political reading of the Bible. The literary reading led many scholars to question the ideology embedded in particular texts. The feminist scholar Trible, for example, says "in the interaction of text and reader, the changing of the second component alters the meaning and power of the first."[18] The time was ripe to challenge not only a historical critical reading of the text but also a pietistic reading that is rooted in separating the church from the state claiming they have two different spheres of responsibility and that the only goal of reading the Bible is to develop a personal relationship with God. In short, some decided to expose violence of power and authority by deconstructing false assumptions and worldviews. Others wanted to consider the response of a community in the Bible and extrapolate its correspondences with a contemporary community in a similar political situation. The main goal is not to interpret the Bible but to interpret life with the help of the Bible.

The Political reading of the Bible, however, is not a new enterprise. Eusebius in the fourth century hails Constantine as the "new Solomon" who builds the new temple, i.e., the church; Cromwell justifies his massacre of Catholics in Drogheda and Wexford by appealing to the slaughter of the Amalekites in 1 Samuel 15. Romans 13 has often been used to justify state violence. Many Palestinian scholars approached the Bible from this perspective. Naim Ateek would be a good Palestinian example for a political reading of the Bible, i.e., Palestinian Liberation theology.

Fifth, we will present now the Palestinian Kairos reading of the Bible. It is fitting now to argue that the Palestinian Kairos Document develops the political reading of the Bible into an ecumenical post-liberal theopolitical reading. It is obvious that the Kairos Document is interested in the contemporary reality. It starts by describing the current painful reality of Palestinians and it even alludes to anti-Palestinianism which is not a private prejudice but an ideological, political, and theological issue. The description of the contemporary reality is done in biblical categories not in a naïve eisegesis that abuses the text nor in a modern exegesis that defer the interests of the reader in the name of finding the authorial intention, but in a healthy dialogue between the contemporary reality and the biblical reality. This dialogue not only makes the biblical reality a contemporary one but also makes the contemporary reality a biblical one. Admittedly, the latter is not divinely inspired but it does have divine presence as long as it is theocentric. The Kairos Document presents unapologetically a theocentric reality that is rooted in God the creator of all and in our savior Jesus Christ, who was born in Bethlehem, lived in Palestine, and died on the cross in Jerusalem. He rose from the dead and ascended to the right hand of God.

18. Trible, "Treasures Old and New," 48–49.

In summary, we need to nourish and celebrate our diversity advocating a theology of humility and willingness to listen to each other. Also we need to present a religious understanding that is not void of mercy, love, or justice. Otherwise we will present an idol not the God depicted in the Scriptures. Hermeneutics cannot be a mere epistemological approach. It is ontological in nature. Interpreting a "sacred text" should lead us not only to a dialogue with the text but also with God who can transform us. As a Christian, the reader must conform to the image of Christ who expressed God's love even to his enemies. This is the approach of the Kairos Document.

A Trinitarian Theology

The Kairos Document boldly affirms a theocentric Trinitarian theology in a context that is dominated by non-Trinitarian perceptions of God, i.e., Judaism and Islam. The core of our Christian identity and uniqueness is embedded in our belief in a triune God: Father, Son, and Holy Spirit. This triune just and good Creator is the basis of human dignity, justice, equality, peace-making, peace-keeping and love. According to the biblical narrative, God not only created Adam and Eve but made them in God's image and likeness. Therefore, the dignity of all human beings is rooted in their identity as God's creatures as they, too, are made in God's own image. However, the human race sinned against God. Consequently, humanity needed a savior. The Kairos Document affirms that this Savior is Jesus Christ. Our Lord Jesus Christ is the Savior, and the Spirit and the church are the journey companions. The Trinitarian conceptual framework allows the Palestinian church to focus on the common grounds among Christians instead of highlighting ecclesiastical differences.

Indeed, a Trinitarian theology starts in Genesis chapter 1 affirming that God is the Creator. The Spirit of God (Gen 1:2) and the Word of God participated in creation (Heb 1:2; John 1:3). Affirming God as our Creator has several implications. We are created in the image of God and sinning against a human being is actually sinning against God. From this point of view, occupation is a sin because it dehumanizes people whom God created. The separation wall, the numerous checkpoints and land-grabbing policies are some of the examples of such dehumanization. Occupation manifests both personal sins and structural injustice. Indeed, occupation is not only a form of political oppression; it is also an insult to God because it insults human beings who are created in the image of God. God is not only their Creator, but also their Father. Genesis chapter 1 points out that all human beings are brothers and sisters, affirming the claim that God is interested in all of his children. In other words, a proper understanding of salvation history does not start with election but with Creation. Creation provides the context for election. Consequently, God is interested in reaching out to the whole world—to God's created family which includes Jews, Christians, Muslims and others. Creation theology enlarges our perception of redemption. The latter includes all of creation, not only human beings. In fact, redemption itself must be seen in creation categories, i.e., new creation. The events of God's redemption are associated with all of God's creation and with a particular land. This chosen land has a universal or cosmic mission.

THEOLOGY OF THE LAND

The first English translation of the Kairos Document avers:

> We believe that our land has a universal mission. In this universality, the meaning of the promises, of the land, of the election, of the people of God open up to include all of humanity, starting from all the peoples of this land. In light of the teachings of the Holy Bible, the promise of the land has never been a political program, but rather the prelude to complete universal salvation. It was the initiation of the fulfillment of the Kingdom of God on earth.[19]

In other words, the election of Abraham is tantamount in its importance to the election of our land.[20] Both have a universal mission. Both are part of God's means to spread his kingdom on earth. Holy space and holy people

---

19. Kairos 2.3. Admittedly, the English translation of the Kairos Document is a good one. Nevertheless, there is room for improvement. I have made few suggestions in the addendum of this book. My suggestions are written in italics. Furthermore, it is important to point out that the English translation of the original Arabic document seems to advocate universalism or the belief that everyone will be saved, but this is neither the intention of the text nor the best interpretation of the Arabic Kairos Document. The Kairos Document does not tackle the various perceptions of soteriology and does not claim that all religions, faiths, and beliefs are salvific. It would have been better to translate the Arabic form as "cosmic" salvation instead of "universal" salvation. At the same time, it is equally important to remember that God is interested in all of his creation, not only human beings. The final outcome will be a new earth.

20. For a biblical response to Christian Zionist theology of the land, see Katanacho, "Christ Is the Owner," 425–41.

must be seen in the context of creation theology that is initiated in the book of Genesis. The kingdom of God is found in the first chapter of Genesis. It is a kingdom that is marked by goodness, blessing, and fruitful land—one that is entrusted to human beings and ordered by holy time. God has already embedded in his kingdom appointed times (*mo'edim*; Gen 1:14) and he has sanctified the Sabbath as a holy time (Gen 2:3).

In the biblical narrative, the election of a land is seen in Genesis 2:8. God planted a garden in a chosen land, Eden. The lives of holy people, Adam and Eve, were shaped by their relationship to Eden. Further, the land in Eden had the power to produce life and death. They either ate from the tree of life or from the tree of the knowledge of good and evil. Eating from the former was allowed, but eating from the latter was forbidden. Unfortunately, humanity ate from the wrong tree and it fell into sin. Their failure to relate to the land properly led not only to their suffering but also to the land's curse. After the fall, earth was cursed and humanity was no longer able to eat from the tree of life as it was no longer accessible.

Humanity lost its Eden. The curse was intensified when Cain killed Abel (Gen 4:11–12). Cain moved away from the presence of the Lord and chose the land of Nod east of Eden (Gen 4:16). Later, the land became a daily burden in the life of Noah (Gen 5:29). Further, during the lifetime of Peleg, the land was divided (Gen 10:25) and humanity made a choice in Genesis 11. They wanted Eretz Shinar (Gen 11:2) but God chose a different land and he wanted to take Abram there (Gen 12:1). Lot joined Abram in looking for God's chosen land. However, when he and his workers had some tension with Abram, Lot decided to choose a different land that seemed to be like the garden of God (Gen 13:10). We know that this was not the land that God had chosen and its end was destruction. In summary, Cain, the builders of Babel and Lot chose lands seeking to find rest, but God had chosen a different land and promised to make it an Eden in spite of its limitations (Isa 51:3; Ezek 36:35).

On the chosen land the way back to Eden would be revealed. Indeed, this revelation was seen in the ministry and life of Jesus Christ. At the cross, he told the repentant thief, "Today you will be with me in Paradise" (Luke 23:43). Christ opened the way back to Paradise through his ministry on earth. In the chosen land there appeared the anointed chosen servant who became the bridge and the road to God's Paradise. All this happened in the Holy Land. So what is the mission of this chosen land in which the road back to paradise is revealed? I will now point out four indispensable areas in the mission of the chosen land. Admittedly, these areas are not explicit in the Kairos Document, but we can extrapolate them from different parts of the document and some of the following concerns were addressed either directly or indirectly in the meetings of the Kairos group.

First, the chosen land is a land of faith. The expression "the land is the fifth gospel" is often heard. This saying is attributed to both Cyril of Jerusalem (315–86) and Jerome (340–420).[21] It reveals the uniqueness of our land. Only in the Holy Land will you find Bethlehem and Jerusalem as well as many other biblical sites. This chosen land has a message to communicate. It teaches people to love the Lord and obey him; without such love there is no rain (Deut 11:13–15). Without rain the land dies and all of its inhabitants suffer. God is clearly the Provider and Sustainer of life in this land. The nature of the land requires trust in God. Further, the stones cry out pointing to God's heart and nature. They share with us the different stories of the heroes of faith and the story of the hero par excellence, Jesus Christ. Consequently, the land continues to help millions of people understand their Bibles and faith in a deeper way. It inspires them to follow Jesus of Nazareth, hear his wisdom and weep with him. Whenever we visit this chosen land, we are reminded of its history and are transformed by its message. Indeed, it is a fifth gospel that has many chapters. Its paragraphs are mountains, valleys, seas, and plains. Its lines and words are holy sites, ancient walls, caves, and streams. The best chapter of the fifth gospel is its connection to Jesus Christ. In this chapter, we see that God entered our world in Israel/Palestine. The person of Christ embodies holy space in which God and man can meet. The land shaped the identity of our Lord and he shaped its identity. The two are related to each other for Christ's humanity is associated with a specific land.

Second, the chosen land is a land of peace. Isaiah informs us that all the nations will come to Jerusalem. There they experience peace. Micah affirms the same message but adds that the vision of peace is associated with a savior that comes out of Bethlehem (Micah 4–5). God declared the divine peace through the birth of Jesus in the fields of Bethlehem (Luke 2:14). Thus, we sing with the angels, "Glory to God in the highest, and on earth peace to men on whom his favor rests" (Luke 2:14). This celestial announcement is not advocating only the peace of Eden that can neither overcome the uproar of sin nor remedy our broken lives nor guarantee an everlasting life. Rather, it is announcing a superior peace that can transform humanity

21. See the introduction to the *Holman Illustrated Study Bible*.

in a troubled earth. This peace is not simply the absence of trouble but is the serene divine presence in spite of humanity's long list of failures. The identity of the chosen land cannot be divorced from the message of the Prince of Peace who came to provide personal and cosmic peace by destroying the power of evil and all the structural injustices. Indeed, the land reminds us not only of the song of the angels but also of the Prince of Peace who fulfilled God's program for bringing peace on earth. Nazareth, Bethlehem, and Jerusalem will continue to advocate a message of peace through the conception and birth, death, and resurrection of Christ. Geography in Palestine has a theological message. The stones are crying out sharing with us salvation history.

Third, it is a land of reconciliation.[22] It hosted the Prince of Peace and its identity is marked with the birth, death and resurrection of Christ. The Kairos Document laments that "Jerusalem, city of reconciliation, has become a city of discrimination and exclusion, a source of struggle rather than peace."[23] The psalmist has described the same city as the city of God in which enemies are transformed into brothers and sisters.[24] The city is the womb in which a new humanity is born. The Kairos Document states that "Jerusalem is at the heart of our reality."[25] It is the place for conceiving a new society in which enmity ends and reconciliation as well as peace dominate. However, today's Jerusalem is marked with conflict and discrimination. Jerusalem has an identity crisis due to its unholy inhabitants.

Fourth, the land is a place of hope for it is the gateway to another dimension. In this land, a star was seen (Matt 2:9) pointing out that Christ had entered the world. Through him heaven opened and angels ascended and descended (John 1:51). Stephen testifies that heavens opened a gateway in Jerusalem (Act 7:55). It is the land that reminds us of heaven's interaction with earth. God has intervened many times in the history of the land in order to conquer the forces of evil. Instead of focusing on salvation history, some are focusing on futurology, or merely expectations about the future and violent apocalyptic scenarios, associating the land with bloodshed and distorting its message of hope. Unfortunately, many wrongly associate the

22. Both Munayer and I have come to the same conclusion but in different ways. Further details are found in Munayer, "Theology of the Land," 234–64.

23. Kairos 1.1.8.

24. For a detailed study of Jerusalem as the city of God, see Katanacho, "Investigating the Purposeful Placement of Psalm 86," 251–55; see also Katanacho, "Jerusalem Is the City of God," 181–99.

25. Kairos 1.1.8

future of the land with Armageddon.[26] It is amazing that the connection between the land and Armageddon sometimes gets more attention than its connection with the birth and resurrection of Christ. The land is the place in which Christ conquered death and rose. It is the place of Pentecost when the Holy Spirit came down and many languages and cultures praised God together. Hope was seen not only in Christ but also in his followers who belonged to many cultures and nations.

Fifth, although the Kairos Document has not addressed this issue, it is good, however, to remember that the chosen land has different parts. It is not a national land but a tribal land and each tribe has to maintain its land as part of her divine inheritance. Each tribe has its own borders. Further, parts of the land are Levitical cities. Other parts are cities of refuge. Ancient Israel did not relate to all the land in the same way. Interestingly, Hebron and Nablus were cities of refuge in biblical times. Today they are inhabited mainly by Palestinians and Jewish settlers are willing to defile these places in order to possess the land. These cities of refuge are no longer accomplishing their calling as a place of refuge and safety.

THEOLOGY OF RESISTANCE

After discussing the theology of the land, it is fitting to address the theology of resistance from the perspective of the Kairos group, i.e., the authors of the Kairos Document. First, the Kairos group is no doubt committed to biblical love. God wants us to love all people, including our enemies. Jesus has told us, "love your enemies and pray for those who persecute you . . . do good to those who hate you" (Matt 5:44; Luke 6:27).[27] Love opens the channels of communication. It should provoke Palestinians and Israelis to talk to each other instead of killing each other. It should help them to pursue justice and security together, for love is not an excuse to abandon justice but an opportunity to pursue it. Second, the Kairos group is committed to justice just like the persistent widow (Luke 18:1–8). She troubled the unjust leaders by insisting on justice. If an unjust judge listened to an insignificant widow, how much more will the just God listen to the cries of the oppressed children and vindicate them. Justice is either administered by God directly (Rom 12:19) or by God's agents who have the authority to punish the evil

26. For a good study of the word "Armaggedon," see Beale, *Book of Revelation*, 838–41.

27. Kairos 4.

doers (Rom 13:4). Revenge and spilling the blood of innocent children is never the Christian way. It must be condemned. Third, the Kairos group is committed to human dignity. All people are created in the image of God (Gen 1:26–27). Thus, anyone who kills another human being attacks God. Killing the children of Israeli settlers is as evil as killing Palestinian children; both are an attack on God. Consequently, both terrorist actions and the occupation are not only sinful acts against human beings but also against God. Terrorism and the occupation dehumanize, stereotype and demonize the creatures of God. The Kairos group states, "The aggression against the Palestinian people which is the Israeli occupation, is an evil that must be resisted. It is an evil and a sin that must be resisted and removed."[28] Sin is not only related to individuals but also to systems. A sinful and oppressive system needs to be resisted with love and nonviolent actions.[29] Fourth, the Kairos group is committed to non-violence. Jesus taught us:

> You have heard that it was said, "Eye for eye, and tooth for tooth." But I tell you, do not resist an evil person. If someone strikes you on the right cheek, turn to him the other also. And if someone wants to sue you and take your tunic, let him have your cloak as well. If someone forces you to go one mile, go with him two miles. (Matt 5:38–41)

The biblical text tells us to resist evil with good (Rom 12:21). Indeed, all Christians are called to resist physical abuse, looting of possessions, and giving up our freedom of choice. Whenever an evil person strikes we must engage that person instead of retaliating in like manner. Whenever the looter steals, we must consider the value of that person in the eyes of God and value him or her more than our possessions. Whenever our freedom is lost due to oppression we must walk the second mile in order to reveal the love of God. Violence breeds violence, but peace–making is the path to a better world. It is the path of Jesus Christ. Fifth, the Kairos group is committed to protecting the children. It is unacceptable to take the lives of Israeli or Palestinian children in the name of a political program or ideology. This is utter evil. Children must have the right to fully develop, to be protected from harmful influences, abuse and exploitation, let alone brutal massacres. We have to build a better future for our Palestinian and

28. Ibid., 4.2.1.

29. The Kairos Document suggests boycott, divestment, and sanctions as some possible nonviolent responses to oppression. We are open to hearing and learning from others on how to resist oppressive actions in nonviolent ways.

Israeli children. Bloodshed is not the right path and state violence must be resisted nonviolently. Sixth, the Kairos group is committed to defending the oppressed. Jesus said, "The Spirit of the Lord is on me, because he has anointed me to preach good news to the poor. He has sent me to proclaim freedom for the prisoners and recovery of sight for the blind, to release the oppressed" (Luke 4:18). The oppressed ones need freedom from evil as well as from its agents who employ oppression to spread a kingdom of violence instead of a kingdom of justice and peace. Seventh, the Kairos group is committed to sharing the land with Israelis in a fair and just political solution. A possible solution might be having two states, one on the land that was occupied by Israel in 1948 and the other on the land that the state of Israel occupied in 1967. Another possible solution might be having one state for all the inhabitants of Israel/Palestine. Politicians might work out the details but theologians should not support any political program that seeks to dehumanize, oppress or rob any human beings of their dignity. We believe that God has allowed both Palestinians and Israelis to live in this land. They both can live in the land either as equal citizens in the same state or in two juxtaposed states. Put differently, a Jew is a gift from God and a Palestinian is also a gift from God. Unless we rejoice in God's gifts, we will continue to exclude and kill one another. The Israeli occupation is a form of violence that contributes to dehumanizing both Palestinians and Israelis. It transforms God's gifts into a curse. Therefore, let us stand together for justice and peace for both Palestinians and Israeli Jews. This leads me to my next point, eschatology.

ESCHATOLOGY

Moltmann argues that Christianity is eschatological.[30] He rightly argues that the promise of the coming kingdom of God at the end of history enables Christian faith to deal with the modern experience of history. The Christian is searching for a new future. In other words, current social and political changes are part of the eschatological process of the coming of the new age. Eschatological orientation empowers people to live with hope. Palestinians are living in a hopeless situation. They are suffering under the Israeli occupation. However, they can still hope in Christ. This hope is the

---

30. Moltman argues that eschatology means the doctrine of Christian hope. It embraces both the object of hope as well as the hope inspired by it. See Moltmann, *Theology of Hope*, 16. See also Harvie, *Jürgen Moltmann's Ethics of Hope*.

bridge that will help us to cross over from the current reality to the hoped-for reality.

Gladly, the Kairos Document does not advocate despair or a belief in an eternal present. It says, "[d]espite the lack of even a glimmer of positive expectation, our hope remains strong."[31] Indeed, it describes a very painful reality, and readers might feel the force of hopelessness as they perceive the current reality through Palestinian eyes. Perhaps, they might be reminded of Dante's famous inscription at the entrance of hell. It says, "Through me you pass into the city of woe . . . All hope abandon ye who enter here."[32] However, like many of the Psalms, the document presents the painful reality in a lament that ends with a deep expression of trust embedded in an eschatological reality.[33] The document states, "[h]ope within us means first and foremost our faith in God and secondly our expectation, despite everything, for a better future."[34] Palestinians are able to escape the tsunami of depression by means of the hope of resurrection – not only the resurrection of the historical Christ but also the resurrection of a divine eschatological reality in which there is hope in a just and good God. This hope is found in the gospel that communicates a message of life rather than destruction and death, and in the church that may seem to be dwindling and weak, yet is like yeast in dough. Its power is not measured by its size, but by its significance.

CONCLUSION

As a coauthor of the Palestinian Kairos Document, I have pointed out some of the explicit points in it and have unpacked some of the implicit assertions. Admittedly, some affirmations were not addressed clearly in the Kairos Document. However, our long discussions in the Kairos group addressed, whether directly or indirectly, most of the aforementioned topics and much more.

It is fitting now to expand the message of hope by looking at Hagar as well as Psalms 42–43.

31. Kairos 3.1.

32. Alighieri, *Divine Comedy*, 13.

33. For further details about the eschatological message of the Psalter, see Katanacho, "Peaceful or Violent Eschatology," 154–72.

34. Kairos 3.2.

five

A Message of Hope

HAGAR FROM A PALESTINIAN PERSPECTIVE

THERE IS NO DOUBT that the biblical figure called Hagar is controversial. First, several Jewish interpreters who interpret Genesis 16 and 21 are either indifferent to Hagar or side with Sarah against her.[1] On the other hand, several African American interpreters are sympathetic to Hagar, giving her a lot of attention.[2] Second, some artists have added to the discord related to Hagar. For example, in front of the Cathedral of Strasbourg stand the thirteenth-century sculptures of Sarah and Hagar. Many Christians throughout the centuries looked at the Strasbourg sculptures and saw Sarah as the victorious queen who holds the cross and cup while Hagar is the defeated woman holding the tablets of the law. The former represents the mother church while the later represents Judaism.[3] This perception is congruent

---

1. Sarah is the wife of Abram. Her name was changed from Sarai to Sarah. This section will use the name Sarah unless it is a direct quotation from primary or secondary sources. It will also use the name Abram even though it was later changed to Abraham.

2. Bailey and Weems are two African American representatives of this trend, while Niditch, Zornberg, and Frymer-Kensky are Jewish interpreters. Bailey, "Hagar," 219–28; Weems, *Just A Sister Away*; Niditch, "Genesis"; Zomberg, *Genesis*; Frymer-Kensky, *In the Wake of the Goddesses*. For further information, see Bailey, "Black and Jewish Women Consider Hagar," 37–44.

3. Pabst, "Interpretations of the Sarah-Hagar Stories," n.p.

with Paul's perception of Hagar in Galatians. He sees Christians as the children of Sarah and the Jews as the children of Hagar (Gal 4:21–31).

Differing from this depiction, in the seventeenth century, Rembrandt "creates the beautiful, stately, and pregnant Hagar next to the bent over old crone, Sarah."[4] Third, several liberation theologians or feminists tend to focus on Hagar's oppression in an androcentric and patriarchal culture, while several conservative Western Evangelicals see Hagar as a mistake that brought trouble and reflected unbelief.[5] Fourth, several prominent Arabic translations of the Bible differ from the King James Bible, the New International Version, and the Revised Standard Version in translating Genesis 16:6.[6] Unlike the pertinent English translations, Arabic translations describe Sarah's action against Hagar as oppressive and humiliating.

Admittedly, these controversies reflect conflicting opinions that are shaped by different presuppositions and social locations. But they also point out the richness of the Hagar figure that continues to provoke the imagination of different peoples from different backgrounds. The story of Hagar in the Old Testament can be perceived from more than one side. Gladly, the apostle Paul has highlighted a very important dimension related to her figure, depicting Hagar as an allegory for the Jews who are in bondage. His interpretation is related to his argument in the epistle to the Galatians. Paul is not claiming that this is the only way to perceive the story of Hagar. He is not, for example, refusing the historical interpretation or the suffering that Hagar endured from Sarah. In short, there are other dimensions to Hagar's rich story that need to be explored.

We hope to add to this spectrum of interpretations by reading the Hagar story from a Palestinian perspective. The section will focus on Hagar's obedience in the context of difficulty. We will first describe the difficulty. Then, we will point out Hagar's transformation in the midst of her ordeal.

---

4. O'Connor, "Abraham's Unholy Family," 26.

5. See, e.g., Trible's feminist depiction or the typical evangelical conservative approach found in Hamilton or Campbell. Trible, "Other Woman," 238; Hamilton, *Handbook on the Pentateuch*, 96–101; Campbell, "Rushing Ahead of God," 276–91.

6. Some of the Arabic translations are *Van Dyck Bible*; *El-Kitab el Muqadas*; and Walton, *Biblia Sacra Polyglotta*. It is worth noting that in Genesis 16, the Living Bible is closer to the Arabic versions.

Hagar's Difficulty

Genesis 16 begins and ends in the Holy Land. In the first part (Gen 16:1–6), we see the rise and fall of Sarah's maid. The first four verses delineate the elevation of Hagar in the following way: she is a maid with a known name (v. 1); she has the potential of producing children (v. 2); she is Abram's wife (v. 3); she is a pregnant wife (v. 4). Hagar's status has been transformed from Sarah's maid into Abram's pregnant wife. However, her joy did not last, for Sarah alters her success into misery. Sarah insists that Hagar is her maid (v. 5) and Abram responds by returning Hagar to his barren wife. The NIV records Abram's conversation with Sarah in the following way: "Your servant is in your hands. . . . Do with her whatever you think best" (Gen 16:6). Abram describes Hagar as Sarah's maid. However, this time she is not the maid that Sarah endorses but the one whom Sarah dethrones. The barren wife seems to be asking Abram for justice (v. 5), but it is more likely that she is pursuing revenge. As soon as Abram releases Hagar into her hands, she oppresses her to the extent that Hagar wants to run away (v. 6) and makes the angel of the Lord describe Hagar's life before escaping, as affliction or misery (Gen 16:11). Obviously, Sarah's actions convinced Hagar that it is better to risk her life and the life of her unborn baby in the wilderness than to stay with her oppressive mistress.

Several English translations downplay Sarah's actions in Genesis 16:6. I have highlighted their translations of the Hebrew verb *ʿānâ*. Following are the translations:

KJV   And when Sarai **dealt hardly** with her, she fled from her face.

RSV   Then Sarai **dealt harshly** with her, and she ran away from her.

NIV   Then Sarai **mistreated** Hagar; so she fled from her.

Contrary to the English translations, several major Arabic translations point out that Sarah humiliated Hagar; further, a sixteenth-century Arabic version agrees with the Living Bible that Sarah tortured Hagar.[7] In fact, the Hebrew word denotes oppression and violence, as well as physical and psychological torture.[8] Seeing Hagar from this perspective, Palestin-

7. The Living Bible translates Gen 16:6 in the following way: "'You have my permission to punish the girl as you see fit,' Abram replied. So Sarai **beat her** and she ran away." I added the bold font.

8. The verb occurs eighty times in the Hebrew Bible and has a range of negative meanings that reflects a strong oppressive nature. For further details, see Even-Soshan,

ians can empathize with her. She lives in the promised land with the family who received the promise. God has promised Abram to give him the land of Canaan (Gen 12:5–7). Concurrently, He commanded him to be a blessing and pointed out that all the nations will be blessed through him (Gen 12:2–3). Abram is supposed to be a blessing to Hagar. Ironically, Hagar was in the promised land with the family that would be the means of blessing the whole world, but she was miserable because of Sarah's sinful behavior and Abram's indifference. The story of Hagar is similar to the struggle of many Palestinians. They, too, are living in the "Promised Land" and are struggling with a group who claim divine rights based on their propinquity to Abram. Sarah's oppressive actions might also be seen in the Palestinian–Israeli conflict. Just like Hagar, some are dethroned, oppressed, and are considered inferior.[9] These difficulties have contributed to increasing Palestinian emigration. The numbers of Palestinian Christians, in particular, are dwindling very fast. Like Hagar, many Palestinian Christians decided to escape from the land.

Hagar's Transformation

After Hagar escapes from the land, the angel of the Lord meets her and speaks to her four times (Gen 16:8, 9, 10, 11). Hagar is instructed to face her difficulties differently. Instead of escaping from the land and the harsh holy family, she should choose to go back. The angel of the Lord said to her, "Go back to your mistress and submit to her" (Gen 16:9). This is not an endorsement of Sarah's oppression but an encouragement to transform our situations by changing our expectations and strategy. Hagar is informed to adopt the same strategy advocated in the Sermon on the Mount. "If someone forces you to go one mile, go with him two miles" (Matt 5:41). By walking the second mile, the oppressed one is challenging the oppressive system in nonviolent ways. In other words, Hagar is called to resist evil with good. She is called to bless the barren Sarah whose seed is supposed to bless the whole world. Sarah might reject Hagar, but she cannot reject her testimony that points to a just God.

Hagar is called to obey God and be a blessing. The blessing that is entrusted into the hands of Hagar can be summarized in two divine attributes:

Konkordantsyah Hadeshah le-Torah, Nevi'im, u-Khetuvim, 901–2; Wegner, "ענה," in VanGemeren, *New International Dictionary*, 3:449–52.

9. For further details, see Burge, *Whose Land?*

the God who hears and the God who sees. First, God hears. The angel of the Lord informed Hagar that her child would be called Ishmael (*yishmāʿ-ĕl*) which means God hears. Ishmael is the answer to Hagar's affliction (Gen 16:11). He would be a living sermon that reminded Hagar of her value in the eyes of God. In Genesis 16, God chooses to speak, not to Abram or Sarah, but to the "inferior" Hagar, for no one can monopolize God. Every time Hagar and Abram call the name Ishmael they will affirm that God hears the cry of the oppressed ones. God heard Hagar's aspirations for freedom by giving her Ishmael who would be a free nomad, not bound by slavery.[10] Through the birth of Ishmael and his numerous seed, Hagar would be transformed from a slave into a matriarch. Hagar's self-understanding was no longer defined by how Sarah viewed her, but by the promises of God.

Similar to Hagar, Palestinian Christians can affirm that God hears their cries.[11] Although, Palestinian Christians who live in Israel and hold its citizenship are second–class citizens in the state of Israel, they are always first–class citizens in the eyes of God. Our perception of our identity is also defined by the promises of God and by an annunciation of a birth of another baby boy, born to affirm that God hears and saves. This baby is Jesus Christ.

The second attribute is the God who sees. Seeing is a clear concern in Genesis 16. In Genesis 16:1–6, or in the "Promised Land," we notice that the verb "see" is mentioned twice and the word "eye" is mentioned three times.[12] Further, in the wilderness or in Genesis 16:7–14, the verb "see" or one of its related forms is repeated four times. When Hagar was in the "Promised Land", her eyes were focused on Sarah. She compared herself to Sarah. On the other hand, Sarah's eyes were on Hagar. She made her the object of humiliation. However, God helped Hagar to stop looking at herself or at Sarah. Instead, the object of Hagar's eyes was *ĕl-Roʾî*, the God who sees or provides. Hagar's experience of God qualified her to be a model, even to the family whom God had chosen to produce the holy seed. Obviously, Hagar goes back to Abram and Sarah telling them about *ĕl-Roʾî* and the angel of the Lord. God chose to send her to the chosen land. Consequently, Abram

---

10. Bar-Efrat, *Narrative Art in the Bible*, 207.

11. The connection between Hagar and Palestinians might also be strengthened if we consider that Muslim tradition sees Hagar as the mother of Ishmael who is the father of arabized Arabs. Although this connection cannot adequately be established biologically or etiologically, the association between Arabs and Ishmael cannot also be completely dismissed.

12. I am referring to the Hebrew text.

names his first born son Ishmael (Gen 16:15). In addition, many years later, Abram becomes like Hagar—in desperate need. The angel of the Lord appears to him, and Abram employs the lessons he has learned from Hagar. He tells his son Isaac that God will provide (*yir'eh*) the sacrifice (Gen 22:8). When God does provide it, Abram calls him Yahweh who provides (y*hwh yir'eh*). Abram uses a divine epithet that is so similar to the one Hagar used.

Thus, Palestinian Christians must turn their eyes away from the difficulties they encounter, and instead, focus on God in whom they believe. Like Hagar, they can be transformed and become a blessing, even to their oppressors. This does not mean endorsing oppression, but it is fighting evil with good. It is also affirming that the election of Abram and Sarah does not justify the oppression of Hagar. Further, Palestinian Christians are in fact the seed of Abraham for they are the followers of Christ and are part of theological Israel. Palestinian Christians, as all followers of Christ, must be willing to walk the second mile because our identity is rooted in the God who hears and our eyes are focused on the God who sees. Indeed, the presence and fellowship of our God can help us to obey God in the context of difficulty. This idea leads me to our last section in which we address the issue of hope from the perspective of Psalms 42, 43, and 73–89.

FROM DEPRESSION TO HOPE

> As the deer pants for streams of water, so my soul pants for you, O God. (Ps 42:1 NIV)

Has the Psalter anything to say to Palestinian refugees? Is it relevant to their loss of land and continual struggle against oppression? The simple answer is yes. In this concluding section, we will explore an ancient voice that addresses a contemporary problem. It is the voice of Psalms 42 and 43. These two psalms should be read together, for both psalms have a similar refrain (Ps 42:5, 11; Ps 43:5) in which a Korahite exhorts himself to move from depression to hope, a topic that is so intriguing to Palestinians. In his despair, the Korahite psalmist is full of questions. He passionately asks God: when will he be able to be in Jerusalem again (Ps 42:2)?

The psalmist's proximity to Jerusalem is a theopolitical concern; to lose Jerusalem is to lose God as well as to be bereft from home. Thus, the enemies of the psalmist taunt him saying, "Where is your God?" (Ps 42:3, 10). They ridicule the psalmist and his seemingly impotent God. Clearly, his present sufferings and his nostalgia indicate a despondent situation. In addition, his tragic sociopolitical reality has theological implications. What should he do and where is his God? The psalmist rightly thinks of his sociopolitical struggles in a theopolitical framework. In this framework, God is interested in all the affairs of human beings and their psychology is a theological concern.[13] Consequently, the psalmist unapologetically, audaciously, as well as sincerely presents his case to God. He is interested in transforming his attitude and emotions toward God in order to restore the peace of his soul and to go back home.

Just like the Korahite psalmist, hundreds of thousands of Palestinians are depressed refugees. Moreover, they fight against injustices and seek to return home. Perhaps, the Korahite psalmist and his theopolitical approach can inspire and empower them. Perhaps, they can learn from his insights. So let us contemplate the divine prudence embedded in his poem. Through his words and attitude, the psalmist communicates two insights that might help Palestinian refugees in their struggle with despair.

First, having the right theology transforms our psychology. The term "theology" is not only associated with orthodoxy (right doctrine) and orthopraxis (right practice) but also with orthopathos. Orthopathos is the kind of human suffering that becomes a source for liberation and social transformation. In his suffering, the psalmist thought that God had forgotten him (Ps 42:9) and even rejected him (Ps 43:2). But in fact, his ordeal made him thirst for God and prompted him to pour himself into prayer. It led him to an intimate relationship with God, the source of true happiness. His heartrending prayer went up to God as a human lament but came back as the message of God to all those who suffer for God's sake. His fervent prayer became God's inspired word. In fact, God made the psalmist an identification figure whose suffering is a divine "megaphone" that "shouts in our pain."[14] God is not silent during, what Anderson calls, the "eclipse of God" or during the catastrophe (*Al Nakbah*) in which hundreds of thousands of Palestinians were forced to leave their homes.[15] God speaks words

13. Terrien, *Psalms*, 356.

14. Lewis, *Problem of Pain*, 91.

15. Anderson and Bishop, *Out of the Depths*, 67.

of comfort to the oppressed and sends messengers personified as light and truth (Ps 43:3) in order to lead those who trust him home and quench their thirst. God will not abandon those who seek him.

This leads us to the second insight: having the right theology, or more specifically the proper view of God, alters the focus of our eschatology. God speaks in and through our pain. In effect, he is transforming the pain of Palestinian refugees into a divine message that reminds the world of the difference between heartless or hardhearted eschatacentric eschatology represented by some Christian theologies and merciful Christocentric eschatology. The former focuses on "God's agenda" or the so called prophetic programs, while the latter reveals God's heart and nature.

In his search for hope the psalmist discovers the God of hope. The psalmist mentions God or one of his epithets twenty-two times.[16] He calls him the living God (Ps 42:2), the God of my life (Ps 42:8), the God of my rock (Ps 42:9), the God of my stronghold (Ps 43:2), and the God of my exceeding joy (Ps 43:4). He finds his hope in an acting God who can be trusted. Thus, the psalmist decides to pray, seeking a just God who will plead his case and prosecute his cunning and wicked oppressors. He wants God to vindicate him (Ps 43:1) and he wishes God to be his lawyer who will present his case and defend him before an ungodly nation. The psalmist no longer seeks to go to Jerusalem to find God, but seeks God to find Jerusalem. The light and truth of God will guide him to God's holy mountain.

A Message of Hope

The insights of the Korahites in Psalms 42–43 did not influence the Asaphites. The latter group laments loosing Jerusalem in Psalms 73–83. The Asaphites developed an exclusive attitude perceiving the nations as enemies. In response to their theology, the Korahites present their second group of psalms (Pss 84, 85, 87, 88).[17] They affirm that finding God is the means to find rest. When we seek the living God first, we will be transformed by his love, justice, and mercy. We will become messengers of the kingdom of God to all the nations. Psalm 87, in particular, helps us to perceive the impact on our lives as we move away from exclusive claims on a particular location to seeking first the kingdom of God. It provides a bold voice that stands in tension with many eschatological systems that lead to polarizing

16. Schökel, "Poetic Structure of Psalm 42–43," 9.

17. The first group is Psalms 42–49.

Israel and her neighbors. It presents to God's people an alternative in which they are not promoting or asking for revenge and blood shed (cf. Ps 79:6, 12). Instead, they join the psalmist of Psalm 87 in having a godly vision for the Egyptians, the Philistines, the people of Tyre, and Cush. They will be born in Zion. The coexistence of Israel with these nations in Zion reflects a biblical voice that stands against xenophobic and inimical attitudes. No more shouts, "Death for the enemies."[18] No more isolation with the "other." No more eschatological programs that favors the Jewish superiority ignoring their calling to be servants of God and light to the nations.

Indeed, Psalm 87 puts before us a vision of equality and an absence of subordination. There are no second-class citizens in Zion. This equality is not just civic but is also covenantal. They all share the same God, are born in the same city, and registered by the same hands.[19] Their linguistic, historical, and military differences are not important. What unites them is God himself. Furthermore, geography is no longer a point of tension for Zion belongs to God, not Israel. It is the city of God and he alone can grant citizenship in his city. The latter is by divine declaration not by biological rights.

This understanding stands in tension with promoting a Jewish Jerusalem or a Jewish state but not necessarily with advocating a truly democratic Israeli state and a shared Jerusalem. In short, instead of promoting a geography that unrealistically calls for isolating the Jews from other ethnic groups, Psalm 87 promotes a new vision of geography in which all can live as equal citizens who are equally concerned to promote justice and righteousness for all.

I believe that the Palestinian Kairos Document captures the vision of Psalm 87, embodies the teachings of biblical love and justice in the Bible, and presents Jerusalem as a symbol of hope for all the inhabitants of Israel/Palestine. Jerusalem provides a conceptual grid in which geography is associated with equality, love, justice, and hope to all. The Palestinian Kairos Document guides us to hope in God and to follow in the footsteps of Jesus Christ. He is the ultimate messenger of justice and love.

Last, at the beginning of this book, I have testified how God has transformed my life and my worldview. I have also presented my understanding

18. For further discussion on Israel's attitude towards the nations, see Smith-Christopher, "Between Ezra and Isaiah."

19. For a helpful discussion of the relationship of earthly and heavenly Jerusalem, see Holwerda, *Jesus and Israel*, 106–12.

of the theology of the land affirming the centrality of Jesus Christ. At the end of this book, I emphasize the value of the Palestinian Kairos Document as a voice of justice and love praying that others will join me as ambassadors of the message of the Palestinian Kairos Document. In his footsteps, I pray that we all continue to advocate biblical hope, love, and justice to both Palestinians and Israeli Jews fighting nonviolently all forms of oppression. An appropriate step would be endorsing the Palestinian Kairos Document. Therefore, I gladly present a revised English translation of Palestinian Kairos Document as an addendum.

Addendum

THE PALESTINIAN
KAIROS DOCUMENT

A Moment of Truth[1]

*A Word of Faith, Hope, and Love
from the Heart of Palestinian Suffering*

INTRODUCTION

WE, A GROUP OF Christian Palestinians, after prayer, reflection and an exchange of opinion, cry out from within the suffering in our country, under the Israeli occupation, with a cry of hope in the absence of all hope; a cry full of prayer and faith in a God ever vigilant, in God's divine providence for all the inhabitants of this land. Inspired by the mystery of God's love for all, the mystery of God's divine presence in the history of all peoples and, in a particular way, in the history of our country, we proclaim our word based

1. I have compared the English translation with the original Arabic text and have made a few minor changes in order to clarify the intended meaning. The important changes are in italics.

on our Christian faith and our sense of Palestinian belonging—a word of faith, hope and love.

Why now? Because today we have reached a dead end in the tragedy of the Palestinian people. The decision-makers content themselves with managing the crisis rather than committing themselves to the serious task of finding a way to resolve it. The hearts of the faithful are filled with pain and with questioning: What is the international community doing? What are the political leaders in Palestine, in Israel and in the Arab world doing? What is the Church doing? The problem is not just a political one. It is a policy in which human beings are destroyed, and this must be of concern to the Church.

We address ourselves to our brothers and sisters, members of our churches in this land. We call out as Christians and as Palestinians to our religious and political leaders, to our Palestinian society and to the Israeli society, to the international community, and to our Christian brothers and sisters in the churches around the world.

1. The Reality on the Ground

1.1 "They say: 'Peace, peace' when there is no peace" (Jer 6:14). These days, everyone is speaking about peace in the Middle East and the peace process. So far, however, these are simply words; the reality is one of Israeli occupation of Palestinian Territories, deprivation of our freedom and all that results from this situation.

1.1.1 The separation wall erected on Palestinian Territory, a large part of which has been confiscated for this purpose, has turned our towns and villages into prisons, separating them from one another, making them dispersed and divided cantons. Gaza, especially after the cruel war Israel launched against it during December 2008 and January 2009, continues to live in inhuman conditions, under permanent blockade and cut off from the other Palestinian Territories.

1.1.2 Israeli settlements ravage our land in the name of God and in the name of force, controlling our natural resources, including water and agricultural land, thus depriving hundreds of thousands of Palestinians, and constituting an obstacle to any political solution.

1.1.3 Reality is the daily humiliation to which we are subjected at the military checkpoints, as we make our way to jobs, schools or hospitals.

1.1.4 Reality is the separation of members of the same family, making family life impossible for thousands of Palestinians, especially where one of the spouses does not have an Israeli identity card.

1.1.5 Religious liberty is severely restricted; the freedom of access to the holy places is denied under the pretext of security. Jerusalem and its holy places are out of bounds for many Christians and Muslims from the West Bank and the Gaza strip. Even Jerusalemites face restrictions during the religious feasts. Some of our Arab clergy are regularly barred from entering Jerusalem.

1.1.6 Refugees are also part of our reality. Most of them are still living in camps under difficult circumstances. They have been waiting for their right of return, generation after generation. What will be their fate?

1.1.7 And the prisoners? The thousands of prisoners languishing in Israeli prisons are part of our reality. The Israelis move heaven and earth to gain the release of one prisoner, but for the thousands of Palestinian prisoners, when will they have their freedom?

1.1.8 Jerusalem is the heart of our reality. It is, at the same time, a symbol of peace and sign of conflict. While the separation wall divides Palestinian neighborhoods, Jerusalem continues to be emptied of its Palestinian citizens, Christians and Muslims. Their identity cards are confiscated, which means the loss of their right to reside in Jerusalem. Their homes are demolished or expropriated. Jerusalem, the city of reconciliation, has become a city of discrimination and exclusion, a source of struggle rather than peace.

1.2 Also part of this reality is the Israeli disregard of international law and international resolutions, as well as the paralysis of the Arab world and the international community in the face of this contempt. Human rights are violated and despite the various reports of local and international human rights' organizations, the injustice continues.

1.2.1 Palestinians within the State of Israel, who have also suffered an historical injustice, although they are citizens and have the rights and obligations of citizenship, still suffer from discriminatory policies. They too are waiting to enjoy full rights and equality like all other citizens in the state.

1.3 Emigration is another element of our reality. The absence of any vision or spark of hope for peace and freedom pushes young people, both Muslim and Christian, to emigrate. Thus the land is deprived of its most important and richest resource—educated youth. The shrinking number of Christians, particularly in Palestine, is one of the dangerous consequences, both of this conflict, and of the local and international paralysis and failure to find a comprehensive solution to the problem.

1.4 In the face of this reality, Israel justifies its actions as self-defense, including occupation, collective punishment and all other forms of reprisals against the Palestinians. In our opinion, this vision is a reversal of reality. Yes, there is Palestinian resistance to the occupation. However, if there were no occupation, there would be no resistance, no fear and no insecurity. This is our understanding of the situation. Therefore, we call on the Israelis to end the occupation. Then they will see a new world in which there is no fear, no threat but rather security, justice and peace.

1.5 The Palestinian response to this reality was diverse. Some responded through negotiations: that was the official position of the Palestinian Authority, but it did not advance the peace process. Some political parties followed the way of armed resistance. Israel used this as a pretext to accuse the Palestinians of being terrorists and was able to distort the real nature of the conflict, presenting it as an Israeli war against terror, rather than an Israeli occupation faced by Palestinian legal resistance aiming at ending it.

1.5.1 The tragedy worsened with the internal conflict among Palestinians themselves, and with the separation of Gaza from the rest of the Palestinian territory. It is noteworthy that, even though the division is among Palestinians themselves, the international community bears an important responsibility for it since it refused to deal positively with the will of the Palestinian people expressed in the outcome of democratic and legal elections in 2006.

Again, we repeat and proclaim that our Christian word in the midst of all this, in the midst of our catastrophe, is a word of faith, hope and love.

2. A Word of Faith: We believe in One God, a Good and Just God.

2.1 We believe in God, one God, Creator of the universe and of humanity. We believe in a good and just God, who loves each one of His creatures. We believe that every human being is created in God's image and likeness and that every one's dignity is derived from the dignity of the Almighty One. We believe that this dignity is one and the same in each and all of us. This means for us, here and now, in this land in particular, that God created us not so that we might engage in strife and conflict but rather that we might come and know and love one another, and together build up the land in love and mutual respect.

2.1.1 We also believe in God's eternal Word, His only Son, our Lord Jesus Christ, whom God sent as the Savior of the world.

2.1.2 We believe in the Holy Spirit, who accompanies the Church and all humanity on its journey. It is the Spirit who helps us to understand Holy Scripture, both Old and New Testaments, showing their unity, here and now. The Spirit makes manifest the revelation of God to humanity, past, present and future.

How Do We Understand the Word of God?

2.2 We believe that God has spoken to humanity, here in our country: "Long ago God spoke to our ancestors in many and various ways by the prophets, but in these last days God has spoken to us by a Son, whom God appointed heir of all things, through whom he also created the worlds" (Heb 1:1–2).

2.2.1 We, Christian Palestinians believe, like all Christians throughout the world, that Jesus Christ came in order to fulfill the Law and the Prophets. He is the Alpha and the Omega, the beginning and the end, and in His light and with the guidance of the Holy Spirit, we read the Holy Scriptures. We meditate upon and interpret Scripture just as Jesus Christ did with the two disciples on their way to Emmaus. As it is written in the Gospel according to Saint Luke: "Then beginning with Moses and all the prophets, he interpreted to them the things about himself in all the scriptures" (Luke 24:27).

2.2.2 Our Lord Jesus Christ came, proclaiming that the Kingdom of God was near. He provoked a revolution in the life and faith of all humanity. He came with "a new teaching" (Mark 1:27), casting a new light on the Old Testament, on the themes that relate to our Christian faith and our daily lives, themes such as the promises, the election, the people of God and the land. We believe that the Word of God is a living Word, casting a particular light on each period of history, manifesting to Christian believers what God is saying to us here and now. For this reason, it is unacceptable to transform the Word of God into letters of stone that pervert the love of God and His providence in the life of both peoples and individuals. This is precisely the error in fundamentalist Biblical interpretation that brings us death and destruction when the word of God is petrified and transmitted from generation to generation as a dead letter. This dead letter is used as a weapon in our present history in order to deprive us of our rights in our own land.

Our Land *Has a Comprehensive Cosmic Mission.*

2.3 We believe that our land has a *cosmic* mission. In this *comprehensiveness*, the meaning of the promises, of the land, of the election, of the people of God open up to include all of humanity, starting from all the peoples of this land. In light of the teachings of the Holy Bible, the promise of the land has never been a political program, but rather the prelude to a *holistic* salvation *of the cosmos*. It was the initiation of the fulfillment of the Kingdom of God on earth.

2.3.1 God sent the patriarchs, the prophets and the apostles to this land so that they might carry forth *to the people of the world a holistic message that includes the cosmos.* Today we constitute three religions in this land, Judaism, Christianity and Islam. Our land is God's land, as is the case with all countries in the world. It is holy inasmuch as God is present in it, for God alone is Holy and Sanctifier. It is the duty of those of us who live here, to respect the will of God for this land. It is our duty to liberate it from the evil of injustice and war. It is God's land and therefore it must be a land of reconciliation, peace and love. This is indeed possible. God has put us here as two peoples, and God gives us the capacity, if we have the will, to live together and establish in it justice and peace, making it in reality God's land: "The earth is the Lord's and all that is in it, the world, and those who live in it" (Ps 24:1).

2.3.2 Our *existence* in this land, as Christian and Muslim Palestinians, is not accidental but rather deeply rooted in the history and geography of this land, resonant with the connectedness of any other people to the land it lives in. It was an injustice when we were driven out. The West sought to make amends for what Jews had endured in the countries of Europe, but it made amends on our account and in our land. They tried to correct an injustice and the result was a new injustice.

2.3.3 Furthermore, we know that certain theologians in the West try to attach a Biblical and theological legitimacy to the infringement of our rights. Thus, the promises, according to their interpretation, have become a menace to our very existence. The "good news" in the Gospel itself has become "a harbinger of death" for us. We call on these theologians to deepen their reflection on the Word of God and to rectify their interpretations so that they might see in the Word of God a source of life for all peoples.

2.3.4 Our connectedness to this land is a natural right. It is not an ideological or a theological question only. It is a matter of life and death. There are those who do not agree with us, even defining us as enemies only because we declare that we want to live as free people in our land. We suffer from the occupation of our land because we are Palestinians. And as Christian Palestinians we suffer from the wrong interpretation of some theologians. Faced with this, our task is to safeguard the Word of God as a source of life and not of death, so that "the good news" remains what it is, "good news" for us and for all. In face of those who use the Bible to threaten our existence as Christian and Muslim Palestinians, we renew our faith in God because we know that the word of God cannot be the source of our destruction.

2.4 Therefore, we declare that any use of the Bible to legitimize or support political options and positions that are based upon injustice, imposed by one person on another, or by one people on another, transform religion into human ideology and strip the Word of God of its holiness, its *inclusiveness* and truth.

2.5 *Therefore*, we also declare that the Israeli occupation of Palestinian land is a sin against God and humanity because it deprives the Palestinians of their basic human rights, bestowed by God. It distorts the image of God in the Israeli who has become an occupier just as it distorts this image in the Palestinian living under occupation. We declare that any theology, seemingly based on the Bible or on faith or on history, that legitimizes the occupation, is far from *the teachings of the Church*, because it calls for violence and holy war in the name of God Almighty, subordinating God to temporary human interests, and distorting the divine image in the human beings living under both political and theological injustice.

3. HOPE

3.1 Despite the lack of even a glimmer of positive expectation, our hope remains strong. The present situation does not promise any quick solution or the end of the occupation that is imposed on us. Yes, the initiatives, the conferences, visits and negotiations have multiplied, but they have not been followed up by any change in our situation and suffering. Even the new U.S. position that has been announced by President Obama, with a manifest desire to put an end to the tragedy, has not been able to make a change in our reality. The clear Israeli response, refusing any solution, leaves no room for positive expectation. Despite this, our hope remains strong, because *God is our hope. He* is good, almighty and loving and His goodness will one day be victorious over the evil in which we find ourselves. As Saint Paul said: "If God is for us, who is against us? . . . Who will separate us from the love of Christ? Will hardship, or distress, or persecution, or famine, or nakedness, or peril, or sword? As it is written, 'For your sake we are being killed all day long' . . . For I am convinced that (nothing) in all creation, will be able to separate us from the love of God" (Rom 8:31, 35, 36, 39).

What Is the Meaning of Hope?

3.2 Hope within us means first and foremost our faith in God and secondly our expectation, despite everything, for a better future. Thirdly, it means not chasing after illusions—we realize that release is not close at hand. Hope is the capacity to see God in the midst of trouble, and to be co-workers with the Holy Spirit who is dwelling in us. From this vision derives the strength to be steadfast, remain firm and work to change the reality in which we find ourselves. Hope means not giving in to evil but rather standing up to it and continuing to resist it. We see nothing in the present or future except ruin and destruction. We see the upper hand of the strong, the growing orientation towards racist separation and the imposition of laws that deny our existence and our dignity. We see confusion and division in the Palestinian position. If, despite all this, we resist this reality today and work hard, perhaps the destruction that looms on the horizon may not come upon us.

Signs of Hope

3.3 The Church in our land, her leaders and her faithful, despite her weakness and her divisions, does show certain signs of hope. Our parish communities are vibrant and most of our young people are active apostles for justice and peace. In addition to the individual commitment, our various Church institutions make our faith active and present in service, love and prayer.

3.3.1 Among the signs of hope are the local centers of theology, with a religious and social character. They are numerous in our different Churches. The ecumenical spirit, even if still hesitant, shows itself more and more in the meetings of our different Church families.

3.3.2 We can add to this the numerous meetings for inter-religious dialogue, Christian-Muslim dialogue, which includes the religious leaders and a part of the people. Admittedly, dialogue is a long process and is perfected through a daily effort as we undergo the same sufferings and have the same expectations. There is also dialogue among the three religions, Judaism, Christianity and Islam, as well as different dialogue meetings on the academic or social level. They all try to breach the walls imposed by the occupation and oppose the distorted perception of human beings in the heart of their brothers or sisters.

3.3.3 One of the most important signs of hope is the steadfastness of the generations, the belief in the justice of their cause and the continuity of memory, which does not forget the "Nakba" (catastrophe) and its significance. Likewise significant is the developing awareness among many Churches throughout the world and their desire to know the truth about what is going on here.

3.3.4 In addition to that, we see a determination among many to overcome the resentments of the past and to be ready for reconciliation once justice has been restored. Public awareness of the need to restore *national and political rights* to the Palestinians is increasing. Jewish and Israeli voices, advocating peace and justice, are raised in support of this with the approval of the international community. True, these forces for justice and reconciliation have not yet been able to transform the situation of injustice, but they have their influence and may shorten the time of suffering and hasten the time of reconciliation.

The Mission of the Church

3.4 Our Church is a Church of people who pray and serve. This prayer and service is prophetic, bearing the voice of God in the present and future. Everything that happens in our land, everyone who lives here, all the pains and hopes, all the injustice and all the efforts to stop this injustice, are part and parcel of the prayer of our Church and the service of all her institutions. Thanks be to God that our Church raises her voice against injustice despite the fact that some desire her to remain silent, closed in her religious devotions.

3.4.1 The mission of the Church is prophetic, to speak the Word of God courageously, honestly and lovingly in the local context and in the midst of daily events. *The Church loves all people.* If she does take sides, it is with the oppressed, to stand alongside them, just as Christ our Lord stood by the side of each poor person and each sinner, calling them to repentance, life, and the restoration of the dignity bestowed on them by God and that no one has the right to strip away.

3.4.2 The mission of the Church is to proclaim the Kingdom of God, a kingdom of justice, peace and dignity. Our vocation as a living Church is to bear witness to the goodness of God and the dignity of human beings. We are called to pray and to make our voice heard when we announce a new society where human beings believe in their own dignity and the dignity of their adversaries.

3.4.3 Our Church *spreads the good news* of the Kingdom, which cannot be tied to any earthly kingdom. Jesus said before Pilate that he was indeed a king but "my kingdom is not from this world" (John 18:36). Saint Paul says: "The Kingdom of God is not food and drink but righteousness and peace and joy in the Holy Spirit" (Rom 14:17). Therefore, religion cannot favor or support any unjust political regime, but must rather promote justice, truth and human dignity. It must exert every effort to purify regimes where human beings suffer injustice and human dignity is violated. The Kingdom of God on earth is not dependent on any political orientation, for it is greater and more inclusive than any particular political system.

3.4.4 Jesus Christ said: "The Kingdom of God is among you" (Luke 17:21). This Kingdom that is present among us and in us is the extension of the mystery of salvation. It is the presence of God among us and our sense of that presence in everything we do and say. It is in this divine presence that we shall do what we can until justice is achieved in this land.

3.4.5 The cruel circumstances in which the Palestinian Church has lived and continues to live have required the Church to clarify her faith and to identify her vocation *in a* better *way.* We have studied our vocation and have come to know it better in the midst of suffering and pain: today, we bear the strength of love rather than that of revenge, a culture of life rather than a culture of death. This is a source of hope for us, for the Church and for the world.

3.5 The Resurrection is the source of our hope .Just as Christ rose in victory over death and evil, so too we are able, as each inhabitant of this land is able, to vanquish the evil of war. We will remain a witnessing, steadfast and active Church in the land of the Resurrection.

4. LOVE: THE COMMANDMENT OF LOVE

4.1 Christ our Lord said: "Just as I have loved you, you also should love one another" (John 13:34). He has already showed us how to love and how to treat our enemies. He said: "You have heard that it was said, 'You shall love your neighbor and hate your enemy.' But I say to you, Love your enemies and pray for those who persecute you, so that you may be children of your Father in heaven; for he makes his sun rise on the evil and on the good, and sends rain on the righteous and on the unrighteous. . . . Be perfect, therefore, as your heavenly Father is perfect" (Matt 5:45–47).

Saint Paul also said: "Do not repay anyone evil for evil" (Rom 12:17). And Saint Peter said: "Do not repay evil for evil or abuse for abuse; but on the contrary, repay with a blessing. It is for this that you were called" (1 Pet 3:9).

Resistance

4.2 This word is clear. Love is the commandment of Christ our Lord to us and it includes both friends and enemies. This must be clear when we find ourselves in circumstances where we must resist evil of whatever kind.

4.2.1 Love is seeing the face of God in every human being. Every person is my brother or my sister. However, seeing the face of God in everyone does not mean accepting evil or aggression on their part. Rather, this love seeks to correct the evil and stop the aggression.

The aggression against the Palestinian people, which is the Israeli occupation, is an evil that must be resisted. It is an evil and a sin that must be resisted and removed. Primary responsibility for this rests with the Palestinians themselves suffering occupation. Christian love invites us to resist it. However, love puts an end to evil by walking in the ways of justice. Responsibility lies also with the international community, because international law regulates relations between peoples today. Finally, responsibility lies with the perpetrators of the injustice; they must liberate themselves from the evil that is in them and the injustice they have imposed on others.

4.2.2 When we review the history of the nations, we see many wars and much resistance to war by war, to violence by violence. The Palestinian people have gone the way of the nations, particularly in the first stages of its struggle with the Israeli occupation. However, it has also engaged in peaceful struggle, especially during the first Intifada. We recognize that all peoples must find a new way in their relations with each other and the resolution of their conflicts. The ways of force must give way to the ways of justice. This applies above all to the peoples that are militarily strong, mighty enough to impose their injustice on the weaker.

4.2.3 We say that our option as Christians in the face of the Israeli occupation is to resist. Resistance is a right and a duty for the Christian. But it is resistance with love as its logic. It is thus a creative resistance for it must find human ways that engage the humanity of the enemy. Seeing the image of God in the face of the enemy means taking up positions in the light of this vision of active resistance to stop the injustice and oblige the perpetrator to end his aggression and thus achieve the desired goal, which is getting back the land, freedom, dignity and independence.

4.2.4 Christ our Lord has left us an example we must imitate. We must resist evil but he taught us that we cannot resist evil with evil. This is a difficult commandment, particularly when the enemy is determined to impose himself and deny our right to remain here in our land. It is a difficult commandment yet it alone can stand firm in the face of the clear declarations of the occupation authorities that refuse our existence and the many excuses these authorities use to continue imposing occupation upon us.

4.2.5 Resistance to the evil of occupation is integrated, then, within this Christian love that refuses evil and corrects it. It resists evil in all its forms with methods that enter into the logic of love and draw on all energies to make peace. We can resist through civil disobedience. We do not resist with death but rather through respect of life. We respect and have a high esteem for all those who have given their lives for our nation. And we affirm that every citizen must be ready to defend his or her life, freedom and land.

4.2.6 Palestinian civil organizations, as well as international organizations, NGOs and certain religious institutions call on individuals, companies and states to engage in divestment and in an economic and commercial boycott of everything produced by the occupation. We understand this to integrate the logic of peaceful resistance. These advocacy campaigns must be carried out with courage, openly sincerely proclaiming that their object is not revenge but rather to put an end to the existing evil, liberating both the perpetrators and the victims of injustice. The aim is to free both peoples from extremist positions of the different Israeli governments, bringing both to justice and reconciliation. In this spirit and with this dedication we will eventually reach the longed-for resolution to our problems, as indeed happened in South Africa and with many other liberation movements in the world.

4.3 Through our love, we will overcome injustices and establish foundations for a new society both for us and for our opponents. Our future and their future are one. Either the cycle of violence will destroy both of us, or peace will benefit both. We call on Israel to give up its injustice towards us, not to twist the truth of reality of the occupation by pretending that it is a battle against terrorism. The roots of "terrorism" are in the human injustice committed and in the evil of the occupation. These must be removed if there be a sincere intention to remove "terrorism". We call on the people of Israel to be our partners in peace and not in the cycle of interminable violence. Let us resist evil together, the evil of occupation and the infernal cycle of violence.

5. Our Word to Our Brothers and Sisters

5.1 We all face, today, a way that is blocked and a future that promises only woe. Our word to all our Christian brothers and sisters is a word of hope, patience, steadfastness and new action for a better future. Our word is that we, as Christians carry a message and we will continue to carry it despite the thorns, despite blood and daily difficulties. We place our hope in God, who will grant us relief in His own time. At the same time, we continue to act in accord with God and God's will, building, resisting evil and bringing closer the day of justice and peace.

5.2 We say to our Christian brothers and sisters: This is a time for repentance. Repentance brings us back into the communion of love with everyone who suffers, the prisoners, the wounded, those afflicted with temporary or permanent handicaps, the children who cannot live their childhood and each one who mourns a dear one. The communion of love says to every believer in spirit and in truth: if my brother is a prisoner I am a prisoner; if his home is destroyed, my home is destroyed; when my brother is killed, then I too am killed. We face the same challenges and share in all that has happened and will happen. Perhaps, as individuals or as heads of churches, we were silent when we should have raised our voices to condemn the injustice and share in the suffering. This is a time of repentance for our silence, indifference, lack of communion, either because we did not persevere in our mission in this land and abandoned it, or because we did not think and do enough to reach a new and integrated vision and remained divided, contradicting our witness and weakening our word. Repentance for our concern with our institutions, sometimes at the expense of our mission, that silenced the prophetic voice given by the Spirit to the Churches.

5.3 We call on Christians to remain steadfast in this time of trial, just as we have throughout the centuries, through the changing succession of states and governments. Be patient, steadfast and full of hope so that you might fill the heart of every one of your brothers or sisters who shares in this same trial with hope. "Always be ready to make your defence to anyone who demands from you an accounting for the hope that is in you" (1 Pet 3:15). Be active and, provided this conforms to love, participate in any sacrifice that resistance asks of you to overcome our present travail.

5.4 Our numbers are few but our message is great and important. Our land is in urgent need of love. Our love is a message to the Muslim and to the Jew, as well as to the world.

5.4.1 Our message to the Muslims is a message of love and of living together and a call to reject fanaticism and extremism. It is also a message to the world that Muslims are neither to be stereotyped as the enemy nor caricatured as terrorists but rather to be lived with in peace and engaged with in dialogue.

5.4.2 Our message to the Jews tells them: Even though we have fought one another in the recent past and still struggle today, we are able to love and live together. We can organize our political life, with all its complexity, according to the logic of this love and its power, after ending the occupation and establishing justice.

5.4.3 The word of faith says to anyone engaged in political activity: human beings were not made for hatred. It is not permitted to hate, neither is it permitted to kill or to be killed. The culture of love is the culture of accepting the other. Through it we perfect ourselves and the foundations of society are established.

6. Our Word to the Churches of the World

6.1 Our word to the churches of the world is firstly a word of gratitude for the solidarity you have shown toward us in word, deed and presence among us. It is a word of praise for the many churches and Christians who support the right of the Palestinian people for self–determination. It is a message of solidarity with those Christians and churches who have suffered because of their advocacy for *truth* and justice.

However, it is also a call to repentance; to revisit fundamentalist theological positions that support certain unjust political options with regard to the Palestinian people. It is a call to stand alongside the oppressed and preserve the word of God as good news for all rather than to turn it into a weapon with which to slay the oppressed. The word of God is a word of love for all His creation. God is not the ally of one against the other, nor the opponent of one in the face of the other. God is the Lord of all and loves all, demanding justice from all and issuing to all of us the same commandments. We ask our sister churches not to offer a theological cover-up for the injustice we suffer, for the sin of the occupation imposed upon us. Our question to our brothers and sisters in the churches today is: are you able to help us get our freedom back, for this is the only way you can help the two peoples attain justice, peace, security and love?

6.2 In order to understand our reality, we say to the churches: come and see. We will fulfill our role to make known to you the truth of our reality, receiving you as pilgrims coming to us to pray, carrying a message of peace, love and reconciliation. You will know the facts and the people of this land, Palestinians and Israelis alike.

6.3 We condemn all forms of racism, whether religious or ethnic, including anti-Semitism and Islamophobia, and we call on you to condemn it and oppose it in all its manifestations. At the same time we call on you to say a word of truth and to take a position of truth with regard to Israel's occupation of Palestinian land. As we have already said, we see boycott and disinvestment as tools of nonviolence for justice, peace and security for all.

7. Our Word to the International Community

7. Our word to the international community is to stop the principle of "double standards" and insist on the international resolutions regarding the Palestinian problem with regard to all parties. Selective application of international law threatens to leave us vulnerable to the law of the jungle. It legitimizes the claims by certain armed groups and states that the international community only understands the logic of force. Therefore, we call for a response to what the civil and religious institutions have proposed, as mentioned earlier: the beginning of a system of economic sanctions and boycott to be applied against Israel. We repeat once again that this is not revenge but rather a serious action in order to reach a just and definitive peace that will put an end to Israeli occupation of Palestinian and other Arab territories and will guarantee security and peace for all.

8. Jewish and Muslim Religious Leaders

8. Finally, we address an appeal to the religious and spiritual leaders, Jewish and Muslim, with whom we share the same vision that every human being is created by God and has been given equal dignity. Hence the obligation for each of us to defend the oppressed and the dignity God has bestowed on them. Let us together try to rise up above the political positions that have failed so far and continue to lead us on the path of failure and suffering.

9. A Call to Our Palestinian People and to the Israelis

9.1 This is a call to see the face of God in each one of God's creatures and overcome the barriers of fear or race in order to establish a constructive dialogue and not remain within the cycle of never-ending manoeuvres that aim to keep the situation as it is. Our appeal is to reach a common vision, built on equality and sharing, not on superiority, negation of the other or aggression, using the pretext of fear and security. We say that love is possible and mutual trust is possible. Thus, peace is possible and definitive reconciliation also. Thus, justice and security will be attained for all.

9.2 Education is important. Educational programs must help us to get to know the other as he or she is rather than through the prism of conflict, hostility or religious fanaticism. The educational programs in place today are infected with this hostility. The time has come to begin a new education that allows one to see the face of God in the other and declares that we are capable of loving each other and building our future together in peace and security.

9.3 Trying to make the state a religious state, Jewish or Islamic, suffocates the state, confines it within narrow limits, and transforms it into a state that practices discrimination and exclusion, preferring one citizen over another. We appeal to both religious Jews and Muslims: let the state be a state for all its citizens, with a vision constructed on respect for religion but also equality, justice, liberty and respect for pluralism and not on domination by a religion or a numerical majority.

9.4 To the leaders of Palestine we say that current divisions weaken all of us and cause more sufferings. Nothing can justify these divisions. For the good of the people, which must outweigh that of the political parties, an end must be put to division. We appeal to the international community to lend its support towards this union and to respect the will of the Palestinian people as expressed freely.

9.5 Jerusalem is the foundation of our vision and our entire life. She is the city to which God gave a particular importance in the history of humanity. She is the city towards which all people are in movement—and where they will meet in friendship and love in the presence of the One Unique God, according to the vision of the prophet Isaiah: "In days to come the mountain of the Lord's house shall be established as the highest of the mountains, and shall be raised above the hills; all the nations shall stream to it . . . He shall judge between the nations, and shall arbitrate for many peoples; they shall beat their swords into ploughshares, and their spears into pruning hooks; nation shall not lift up sword against nation, neither shall they learn war any more" (Isa 2:2–5). Today, the city is inhabited by two peoples of three religions; and it is on this prophetic vision and on the international resolutions concerning the totality of Jerusalem that any political solution must be based. This is the first issue that should be negotiated because the recognition of Jerusalem's sanctity and its message will be a source of inspiration towards finding a solution to the entire problem, which is largely a problem of mutual trust and ability to set in place a new land in this land of God.

10. Hope and Faith in God

10. In the absence of all hope, we cry out our cry of hope. We believe in a *Good and Just* God. We believe that God's goodness will finally triumph over the evil of hate and of death that still persist in our land. We will see here "a new land" and "a new human being," capable of rising up in spirit to love each one of his or her brothers and sisters.

Bibliography

Alighieri, Dante. *The Divine Comedy of Dante Alighieri*. Translated by Henry Francis Cary. Whitefish, MT: Kessinger, 2004.

Al-Kitab al Muqadas. Lebanon: Bible Society, 1995.

Allen, Leslie. *Ezekiel 20–48*. Word Biblical Commentary 29. Libronix Digital Library System 3.0f. Logos Bible Software. Nashville: Thomas Nelson, 2002.

Allen, Ronald. "Numbers." In *Expositor's Bible Commentary*, edited by Frank E. Gaebelein, 2:655–1008. Grand Rapids: Zondervan, 1990.

Anderson, Bernhard, and Steven Bishop. *Out of the Depths: The Psalms Speak for Us Today*. 3rd ed. Louisville: Westminster John Knox, 2000.

Aune, David. *Revelation 1–5*. Word Biblical Commentary 52a. Libronix Digital Library System 3.0f. Logos Bible Software. Nashville: Thomas Nelson, 2002.

Bailey, Kenneth. "St. Paul's Understanding of the Territorial Promise of God to Abraham: Rom 4:13 in Its Historical and Theological Context." *Theological Review: Near East School of Theology* 15 (1994) 59–69.

Bailey, Wilma. "Black and Jewish Women Consider Hagar." *Encounter* 63 (2002) 37–44.

———. "Hagar: A Model for an Anabaptist Feminist?" *Mennonite Quarterly Review* 68 (1994) 219–28.

Bar-Efrat, Shimon. *Narrative Art in the Bible*. Translated by Dorothea Shefer-Vanson. JSOT Supplement Series 70. Sheffield, UK: Almond, 1989.

Barton, John. "Historical-Critical Approaches." In *Biblical Interpretation*, edited by John Barton, 9–20. Cambridge: Cambridge University Press, 1998.

Beale, G. K. *The Book of Revelation: A Commentary on the Greek Text*. Grand Rapids: Eerdmans, 1999.

Biyela, M. D. "Beyond the Kairos Document: Christology for a Post-Apartheid South Africa." PhD diss., Luther Northwestern Theological Seminary, 1994.

Boice, James Montgomery. "Galatians." In *Expositor's Bible Commentary*, edited by Frank E. Gaebelein, 10:407–508. Grand Rapids: Zondervan, 1976.

The Book of Jubilees. Translated by R. H. Charles. London: Society for Promoting Christian Knowledge. No pages. Online: http://www.sacred-texts.com/bib/jub.

Boyer, Paul. *When Time Shall Be No More: Prophecy Belief in Modern American Culture*. Cambridge: Harvard University Press, 1992.

Brueggemann, Walter. *The Land: Place as Gift, Promise, and Challenge in Biblical Faith*. 2nd ed. Minneapolis: Fortress, 2002.

Burge, Gary. *Jesus and the Land: The New Testament Challenge to "Holy Land" Theology*. Grand Rapids: Baker, 2010.

———. *Whose Land? Whose Promise?* Cleveland: Pilgrim, 2003.

Burns, J. Lanier. "Israel and the Church of a Progressive Dispensationalist." In *Three Central Issues in Contemporary Dispensationalism: A Comparison of Traditional and Progressive Views*, edited by Herbert Bateman IV, 263–303. Grand Rapids: Kregel, 1999.

Bush, Frederic. *Ruth, Esther*. Word Biblical Commentary 9. Libronix Digital Library System 3.of. Logos Bible Software. Nashville: Thomas Nelson, 2002.

Campbell, George Van Pelt. "Rushing Ahead of God: An Exposition of Genesis 16:1–16." *Bibliotheca sacra* 163 (2006) 276–91.

Carson, D. A. "Matthew." In *Expositor's Bible Commentary*, edited by Frank E. Gaebelein, 8:1–599. Grand Rapids: Zondervan, 1984.

Chacour, Elias, and David Hazard. *Blood Brothers*. 2nd ed. Grand Rapids: Chosen, 2003.

Chafer, Lewis. *Systematic Theology*. Vol. 4. Dallas: Dallas Seminary Press, 1948.

Cooper, Lamar. *Ezekiel*. The New American Commentary 17. Libronix Digital Library System 3.of. Logos Bible Software. Nashville: Broadman & Holman, 2001.

Cragg, Kenneth. *The Arab Christian: A History in the Middle East*. Louisville: John Knox, 1991.

Crutchfield, Larry. *The Origins of Dispensationalism: The Darby Factor*. Lanham, MD: University Press of America, 1992.

Dallas Theological Seminary. "Article XX—The Second Coming of Christ." No pages. Online: http://www.dts.edu/about/doctrinalstatement/.

Davies, W. D. *The Gospel and the Land: Early Christianity and Jewish Territorial Doctrine*. Berkeley: University of California Press, 1974.

———. *The Territorial Dimension of Judaism*. Berkeley: University of California Press, 1982.

Dunn, James. *Romans 1–8*. Word Biblical Commentary 38a. Libronix Digital Library System 3.of. Logos Bible Software. Nashville: Thomas Nelson, 2002.

Ehlert, Arnold. *A Bibliographic History of Dispensationalism*. Grand Rapids: Baker, 1965.

Ellingworth, Paul. *The Epistle to the Hebrews: A Commentary on the Greek Text*. Grand Rapids: Eerdmans, 1993.

Eph'al, Israel. *The Ancient Arabs: Nomads on the Borders of the Fertile Crescent, 9th–5th Centuries B.C.* Leiden: Brill, 1982.

Even-Soshan, Avraham. *Konkordantsyah Hadeshah le-Torah, Nevi'im, u-Khetuvim*. Jerusalem: Kiryat Sefer, 1982.

Falwell, Jerry. *Listen, America!* New York: Doubleday, 1980.

———. "The Twenty-First Century and the End of the World." *Fundamentalism Journal* 7 (1988) 10–11.

Fensham, F. Charles. *The Books of Ezra and Nehemiah*. New International Commentary on the Old Testament. Grand Rapids: Eerdmans, 1982.

Frymer-Kensky, Tikva. *In the Wake of the Goddesses*. New York: Fawcett Columbine, 1992.

Ganzel, Tova. "The Descriptions of the Restoration of Israel in Ezekiel." *Vetus Testamentum* 60 (2010) 197–211.

Grenz, Stanley, and John Franke. *Beyond Foundationalism: Shaping Theology in a Postmodern Context*. Louisville: Westminster John Knox, 2001.

Gundry, Robert. *Matthew: A Commentary on His Literary and Theological Art*. Grand Rapids: Eerdmans, 1982.

Habel, Norman. *The Land Is Mine: Six Biblical Land Ideologies*. Overtures to Biblical Theology. Minneapolis: Fortress, 1995.

Hagner, Donald. *Matthew 14–28*. Word Biblical Commentary 33b. Dallas: Word, 1995.

Hamilton, Victor. *The Book of Genesis: Chapters 1–17*. New International Commentary on the Old Testament. Grand Rapids: Eerdmans, 1990.

———. *Handbook on the Pentateuch*. Grand Rapids: Baker, 1982.

Harvie, Timothy. *Jürgen Moltmann's Ethics of Hope: Eschatological Possibilities for Moral Action*. Farnham, UK: Ashgate, 2009.

Hedding, Malcolm. "Christian Zionism 101: Giving Definition to the Movement." International Christian Embassy Jeruslam. No Pages. Online: http://int.icej.org/media/christian-zionism-101.

Holman Illustrated Study Bible. Nashville: Holman, 2006.

Holwerda, David. *Jesus and Israel: One Covenant or Two?* Grand Rapids: Eerdmans, 1995.

Hornstra, Willem. "Christian Zionism Among Evangelicals in the Federal Republic of Germany." PhD diss., University of Wales, 2007.

Hornstra, Wilrens. "Western Restorationism and Christian Zionism: Germany as a Case Study." In *Christian Perspectives on the Israeli-Palestinian Conflict*, edited by Wesley Brown and Peter Penner, 131–48. Schwarzenfeld, Germany: Neufeld, 2008.

Hughes, Robert, and J. Carl Laney. *Tyndale Concise Bible Commentary*. Libronix Digital Library System 3.0f. Logos Bible Software. Wheaton: Tyndale House, 2001.

Jamieson, Robert, et al. *A Commentary, Critical and Explanatory, on the Old and New Testaments*. Libronix Digital Library System 3.0f. Logos Bible Software. Nashville: Logos Research System, 1997.

Janzen, W. "Land." In *Anchor Bible Dictionary*, edited by David Noel Freedman, 4:143–54. New York: Doubleday, 1992.

Japhet, Sara. *I & II Chronicles: A Commentary*. Old Testament Library. Louisville: Westminster John Knox, 1993.

Juster, Daniel. "Dry Bones and Israel's Restoration." Tikkun International. No pages. Online: http://www.tikkunministries.org/ENL/nl-julaug06.htm.

Kallai, Zecharia. "The Patriarchal Boundaries, Canaan and the Land of Israel: Patterns and Application in Biblical Historiography." *Israel Exploration Journal* 47 (1997) 69–82.

Kassis, Rifat, et al. "A Moment of Truth: A Word of Faith, Hope, and Love from the Heart of Palestinian Suffering." Kairos Palestine, 2009. Online: http://www.kairospalestine.ps/sites/default/Documents/English.pdf.

Katanacho, Yohanna. "Christ Is the Owner of Haaretz." *Christian Scholar's Review* 34 (2005) 425–41.

———. "The Christian and Ramadan." *Al-Liqa' Journal* 36 (2011) 102–6.

———. "Investigating the Purposeful Placement of Psalm 86." PhD diss., Trinity International University, 2007.

———. "Jerusalem Is the City of God: A Palestinian Reading of Palm 87." In *The Land Cries Out*, edited by Salim Munayer and Lisa Loden, 181–99. Eugene, OR: Wipf & Stock, 2012.

———. "The Label Arab in the Old Testament." *Middle East Association for Theological Education Journal* 5 (2010) 1–11.

———. "Lahoot Aher al-Ayyam min Minthar Filsteeni" (Eschatology from a Palestinian perspective). *Al-Liqa* 24 (2009) 106–16.

———. "Palestinian Protestant Theological Responses to a World Marked by Violence." *Missiology: An International Review* 36 (2008) 289–305.

———. "Peaceful or Violent Eschatology: A Palestinian Christian Reading of the Psalter." In *Christ at the Checkpoint: Theology in the Service of Justice and Peace*, edited by Paul Alexander, 154–72. Eugene, OR: Wipf & Stock, 2012.

Kittel, Gerhard, and Gerhard Friedrich, editors. *Theological Dictionary of the New Testament: Abridged in One Volume.* Translated by Geoffrey Bromiley. Libronix Digital Library System 3.of. Logos Bible Software. Grand Rapids: Eerdmans, 1995.

Knauth, R. J. D. "Alien, Foreign Resident." In *Dictionary of the Old Testament Pentateuch,* edited by T. Desmond Alexander and David Baker, 26–33. Downers Grove, IL: InterVarsity, 2003.

Koester, Craig R. *Hebrews: A New Translation with Introduction and Commentary.* Anchor Bible 36. New York: Doubleday, 2001.

Kreider, Dallas. "Darby, John Nelson." In *The Encyclopedia of Protestantism,* edited by Hans J. Hillerbrand, 549–51. London: Routledge, 2004.

Lewis, C. S. *The Problem of Pain.* New York: HarperCollins, 2001.

Loden, Lisa, et al., editors. *The Bible and the Land.* Jerusalem: Musalaha, 2000.

Meadowcroft, Tim. *Message of the Word of God: The Glory of God Made Known.* Downers Grove, IL: InterVarsity, 2011.

Merkley, Paul. *Christian Attitudes towards the State of Israel.* Montreal: McGill-Queen's University Press, 2001.

Merrill, Eugene. *Deuteronomy.* New American Commentary 4. Libronix Digital Library System 3.of. Logos Bible Software. Nashville: Broadman and Holman, 2001.

Moltmann, Jürgen. *Theology of Hope: On the Ground and the Implications of a Christian Eschatology.* New York: Harper & Row, 1967.

Morris, Leon. "Hebrews." In *Expositor's Bible Commentary,* edited by Frank E. Gaebelein, 12:1–158. Grand Rapids: Zondervan, 1981.

Munayer, Salim. "Theology of the Land: From a Land of Strife to a Land of Reconciliation." In *The Land Cries Out,* edited by Salim Munayer and Lisa Loden, 234–64. Eugene, OR: Wipf & Stock, 2012.

Niditch, Susan. "Genesis." In *The Women's Bible Commentary,* edited by Carol Newsom and Sharon Ringe, 13–29. Louisville: Westminster John Knox, 1998.

O'Connor, Kathleen. "Abraham's Unholy Family: Mirror, Witness, Summons." *Journal for Preachers* 21 (1997) 26–34.

Pabst, Irene. "The Interpretation of the Sarah-Hagar Stories in Rabbinic and Patristic Literature: Sarah and Hagar as Female Representations of Identity and Difference." Online: http://www.lectio.unibe.ch/03_1/pabst.pdf.

Petersen, R. M. "Time, Resistance and Reconstruction: Rethinking Kairos Theology." PhD diss., University of Chicago, 1996.

Pritchard, James E. *Ancient Near Eastern Texts Relating to the Old Testament.* Princeton: Princeton University Press, 1955.

Retsö, Jan. *Arabs in Antiquity: Their History from the Assyrians to the Umayyads.* London: RoutledgeCurzon, 2002.

Rad, Gerhard von. *The Problem of the Hexateuch and Other Essays.* Translated by E. W. Trueman Dicken. New York: McGraw Hill, 1966.

Ryrie, Charles. *Dispensationalism Today.* Chicago: Moody, 1965.

Sabella, Bernard. "Religious and Ethnic Communities." In *Encyclopedia of the Palestinians,* edited by Philip Mattar, 346–49. New York: Facts on File, 2000.

Sarna, Nahum. *Exodus.* Jewish Publication Society Torah Commentary. Philadelphia: Jewish Publication Society, 1991.

Schökel, Alonso. "The Poetic Structure of Psalm 42–43." *Journal for the Study of the Old Testament* 1 (1976) 4–11.

Seitz, Christopher. "Ezekiel 37:1–14." *Interpretation* 46 (1992) 53–56.

Shahid, Irfan. *Byzantium and the Arabs in the Fifth Century*. Washington, DC: Dumbarton Oaks Research Library and Collection, 2006.

———. *Byzantium and the Arabs in the Fourth Century*. Washington, DC: Dumbarton Oaks Research Library and Collection, 2006.

———. *Byzantium and the Arabs in the Sixth Century*. Washington, DC: Dumbarton Oaks Research Library and Collection, 2009.

———. *Rome and the Arabs: A Prolegomenon to the Study of Byzantium and the Arabs*. Washington, DC: Dumbarton Oaks Research Library and Collection, 1984.

Sizer, Stephen. "Dispensational Approaches to the Land." In *The Land of Promise*, edited by Philip Johnston and Peter Walker, 142–71. Downers Grove, IL: InterVarsity, 2000.

———. *Zion's Christian Soldiers? The Bible, Israel, and the Church*. Nottingham, UK: InterVarsity, 2007.

Smith, Eli, and Cornelius V. A. Van Dyck. *Arabic Van Dyck Bible*. Cairo: Bible Society of Egypt, 1999.

Smith-Christopher, Daniel L. "Between Ezra and Isaiah: Exclusion, Transformation, and Inclusion of the 'Foreigner' in Post-Exilic Biblical Theology." In *Ethnicity and the Bible*, edited by Mark G. Brett, 117–42. Biblical Interpretation Series 19. Leiden: Brill, 1996.

"The South African Kairos Document." Online: http://www.sahistory.org.za/pages/library-resources/officialdocs/kairos-document.htm.

Sparks, Kenton. *Ethnicity and Identity in Ancient Israel: Prolegomena to the Study of Ethnic Sentiments and Their Expression in the Hebrew Bible*. Winona Lake, IN: Eisenbrauns, 1998.

Spence-Jones, H. D. M. *Genesis*. Pulpit Commentary. Libronix Digital Library System 3.0f. Logos Bible Software. Logos Research System, 2004.

———. *Isaiah*. Vol. 2. Pulpit Commentary. Libronix Digital Library System 3.0f. Logos Bible Software. Logos Research System, 2004.

Strong, John. "Egypt's Shameful Death and the House of Israel's Exodus from Sheol." *Journal for the Study of the Old Testament* 34 (2010) 475–504.

Tarazi, Paul. *Land and Covenant*. St. Paul, MN: Orthodox Center for the Adavancement of Biblical Studies, 2009.

Terrien, Samuel. *The Psalms: Strophic Structure and Theological Commentary*. Grand Rapids: Eerdmans, 2003.

Townsend, Jeffrey. "Fulfillment of the Land Promise in the Old Testament." *Bibliotheca Sacra* 142 (1985) 320–37.

Trible, Phyllis. "The Other Woman: A Literary and Theological Study of the Hagar Story." In *Understanding the Word: Essays in Honor of Bernhard W. Anderson*, edited by James Butler et al., 221–46. JSOT Supplement Series 37. Sheffield, UK: JSOT, 1985.

———. "Treasures Old and New: Biblical Theology and the Challenge of Feminism." In *The Open Text: New Directions for Biblical Studies?*, edited by Francis Watson, 32–56. London: SCM, 1993.

Trimingham, J. Spencer. *Christianity among the Arabs in Pre-Islamic Times*. New York: Seabury, 1979.

Van der Water, Desmond P. "The Legacy of a Prophetic Movement: A Socio-Theological Study of the Reception and Response to the Kairos Document." PhD diss., University of Natal, 1998.

VanGemeren, Willem, editor. *New International Dictionary of Old Testament Theology and Exegesis*. 5 vols. Grand Rapids: Zondervan, 1997.

Bibliography

Vaughan, Curtis. "Colossians." In *Expositor's Bible Commentary*, edited by Frank E. Gaebelein, 11:161–226. Grand Rapids: Zondervan, 1978.

Villa-Vicencio, Charles, editor. *Theology & Violence: The South African Debate*. Grand Rapids: Eerdmans, 1987.

Volf, Miroslav. "Theology, Meaning & Power: A Conversation with George Lindbeck on Theology & the Nature of Christian Difference." In *The Nature of Confession: Evangelicals and Postliberals in Conversation*, edited by Timothy Phillips and Dennis Okholm, 45–66. Downers Grove, IL: InterVarsity, 1996.

Walker, Peter. "The Land in the Apostles' Writings." In *The Land of Promise*, edited by Philip Johnston and Peter Walker, 81–99. Downers Grove, IL: InterVarsity, 2000.

Walton, Brian. *Biblia Sacra Polyglotta: Tomus Primus*. Graz, Austria: Akademische Druck-u., 1963.

Walvoord, John. "The Amazing Rise of Israel!" *Moody Monthly* 68 (1967) 22–25.

———. *Major Bible Prophecies: 37 Crucial Prophecies that Affect You Today*. Grand Rapids: Zondervan, 1991.

Watts, John. *Isaiah 34–66*. Word Biblical Commentary 25. Libronix Digital Library System 3.of. Logos Bible Software. Nashville: Thomas Nelson, 2002.

Wazana, Nili. *All the Boundaries of the Land: The Promised Land in Biblical Thought in Light of the Ancient Near East*. Jerusalem: Bialik, 2007.

———. "From Dan to Beer-Sheba and from the Wilderness to the Sea: Literal and Literary Images of the Promised Land in the Bible." In *Experiences of Place*, edited by Mary MacDonald, 45–85. Cambridge: Center for the Study of World Religions, 2003.

Weems, Renita. *Just a Sister Away: A Womanist Vision of Women's Relationships in the Bible*. San Diego: LuraMedia, 1988.

Weinfeld, Moshe. *The Promise of the Land: The Inheritance of Canaan by the Israelites*. Berkeley: University of California Press, 1993.

Wenham, Gordon. *Genesis 1–15*. Word Biblical Commentary 1. Libronix Digital Library System 3.of. Logos Bible Software. Nashville: Thomas Nelson, 2002.

Wright, Christopher. *The Message of Ezekiel: A New Heart and a New Spirit*. The Bible Speaks Today. Downers Grove, IL: Zondervan, 2001.

Zomberg, Avivah. *Genesis: The Beginning of Desire*. Philadelphia: Jewish Publication Society, 1995.

Made in United States
Cleveland, OH
01 July 2025

18107808R00066